Out of the Mud & Mire

Out of the Mud & Mire
Rising from the Depths of Despair

BRITTANY N. ROBERTS

Suffolk, Virginia

Out of the Mud & Mire:
Rising from the Depths of Despair

Copyright © 2020 by Brittany N. Roberts
All rights reserved.

All rights reserved. This book is protected by the copyright laws of the United States of America. This book may not be copied or reprinted for commercial gain or profit. The use of quotations or occasional page copying for personal or group study is permitted and encouraged. Permission will be granted upon request.

Final Step Publishing, LLC

PO Box 1441
Suffolk, VA 23439

Soft cover ISBN: 978-1-7349784-5-2

For Worldwide Distribution. Printed in U.S.A.

This book is dedicated to anyone
who has ever struggled to see the Light
in their darkest night.

May God, the inspiration and fountain of hope, fill you to overflowing with uncontainable joy and perfect peace as you trust in Him. And may the power of the Holy Spirit continually surround your life with his super-abundance until you radiate with hope!
(Romans 15:13 TPT)

Contents

Introduction 8

Part 1
The Mud & Mire: *Acknowledging Your Despair*

Chapter 1. Addressing the Pain 15
Chapter 2. Naming the Pain 27
Chapter 3. Sitting in Darkness 41

Part 2
Waiting on God: *Actively Uncovering the Pain*

Chapter 4. Get Up Child 59
Chapter 5. Asking the Hard Questions 69
Chapter 6. Surrendering 81
Chapter 7. Fighting 91

Part 3
The Lifting: *Essential Tools Needed*

Chapter 8. A Transformed Mind 107
Chapter 9. Community 119
Chapter 10. The Word of God 139
Chapter 11. Prayer 159

Part 4
Standing on Solid Ground: *Walking in Freedom*

Chapter 12. A New Song 175
Chapter 13. Rehearse & Repeat 193

Acknowledgments 203

Introduction

I can't do this anymore, I muttered to a God that I was starting to doubt even existed. *What have I done? Why is this happening to me?* I sat on the bathroom floor in my apartment crying, confused, and convinced that it would just be better to end my life. I couldn't take it anymore. I began throwing out ultimatums, like *God if you really exist or really care about me, you need to show me, or I'm done.* I even went as far as telling God if He didn't speak to me that night then I was going to do it. I was going to take my life.

Have you ever been there? Have you ever felt like your hope, your peace, and your joy was stolen from you? Like it was a struggle to get out of bed every day? Like you were stuck in this dark place with no idea on earth how you ended up there or how to get out? Like it was better to just end your life? This is exactly how I felt for years. It wasn't always that way though. It kind of felt like it came out of nowhere. One day I was living and enjoying college life, and the next I was stuck in this deep, dark pit.

Here it is (currently 2020) and as you can tell, God did speak to me because you are reading this book. Truth is, I've experienced some of the lowest moments in my life, and at first, I had no idea how to navigate through them. Instead I coped with it, found things to fill the void, and eventually tried burying the pain thinking that was the solution. But it wasn't. It was the worst thing that I could have done. And, sure, burying the pain worked for a while, but eventually it began to resurface in every aspect of my life leaving me desperate for a way out. It was the very thing that almost cost me my life.

This is why I am writing to you today. I know there are many people out there who are hurting. Who are questioning their worth. Wondering who truly cares. Wondering if their pain will ever stop. Wondering if they will ever be free. Wondering if they could ever get away from the darkness they feel. Maybe you're that very person. I was there, and I have been there many times in my life.

But God, by His amazing grace, picked me up each time when I was most desperate. He showed me that He cares, and if it were not for Him, I honestly would not be here today. He gave me a message that has transformed my life and while I could keep it to myself, I am choosing to share it with whoever picks up this book.

The Meaning of the Title

Now, it was about March 2018 when God laid the title of this book on my heart, and boy was I blown away. It comes straight from Psalm 40 verse 1 and 2 which states,

> "I waited and waited and waited some more, patiently, knowing God would come through for me. Then, at last, he bent down and listened to my

cry. He stooped down to lift me out of danger from the desolate pit I was in, out of the muddy mess I had fallen into. Now he's lifted me up into a firm, secure place and steadied me while I walk along his ascending path" (Psalm 40:1-2 TPT).

I resonated so much with David's words. I thought, *this is me! This is my story!*
Google dictionary defines *mire* as a situation or state of difficulty, distress, or embarrassment from which it is hard to extricate oneself. And I'm sure you already know what mud is.
The title *Out of the Mud & Mire* comes exactly from this psalm of David. It is a testimony of how God lifted David in a time that he was seemingly stuck in a low place, a "pit." This is one of the same testimonies that I have the privilege to share with you. As I reflected on events in my life, I found that there were many practical things that I had to do and still do today that essentially help me to navigate those dark, miry places of life.
So, my sincere hope is that the tools discussed in these chapters will guide you in those dark, miry places and teach you how to transcend the bad, the ugly, the lowest, and the hopeless moments in life. I cannot promise or guarantee that your life will drastically change after reading this book. Nor can I guarantee that it is the best approach to your healing. But I do hope that *Out of the Mud & Mire* encourages you to keep fighting and seeking God when all you think, see, or feel is darkness. Not only this, I hope it shows you how God can lift you amid your despair, just like He lifted me. As you read through the pages of this book, I encourage you and even pray that you would invite

the Holy Spirit into your space. I pray that your eyes, ears, heart, and mind would be open to the work that God wants to do in your life. So, let's dive in.

PART 1

The Mud & Mire:
Acknowledging Your Despair

Chapter 1

Addressing the Pain

Has God ever spoken to you in a way that was so clever yet so simple? This is exactly what He did one day as I was making pancakes for breakfast. Let me explain. One day I had gotten home from the gym and I wanted some pancakes after my workout, so I whipped out my batter and everything else then proceeded to make them.

The first pancake I made was absolutely beautiful. It was the perfect size, golden brown, and fluffy just like how my mom would make them. I'll be honest, I was proud at that moment because my pancakes typically come out looking, well, not so perfect. (They still tasted good though.) Well, I went to make two more pancakes and this time they were slightly burned. However, I didn't throw them away. Instead, I hid them on the bottom of my pancake stack. After that, I buttered my stack of pancakes, lightly drizzled them with syrup, perfectly centered them on my plate, and added some fruit to the side.

I took out my phone, snapped a quality picture, and then I posted it on Instagram because I needed every one of my followers to see my perfect stack. I mean it looked like one of those fancy gourmet meals, so of course, I just had to show it off. Once that was done and posted, I sat down to enjoy my pancakes. It was at that moment that I felt God speaking. He didn't even let me get a bite in before He came for my whole life.

He basically told me that this is the same thing that I was doing with my pain. Hiding it. On the outside (the top pancake) I made it appear like I was put together and fine, but inside (the pancakes on the bottom), I was far from it. I was faking it. I paraded around every day like I was good because I didn't want people to know what I was really struggling with inside. I only posted to make my life look good. I didn't want to show any weakness. But the truth is that I was hurting. I could've crumbled at any moment, but I continuously whispered to myself, *keep it together Brittany. You got this.*

I imagine that maybe you can resonate with me a little. That you, too, can think of a time, experience, or thing that you have hidden. Maybe there is something currently that you are hiding from the world and for whatever reason, you are afraid to show that weakness? Maybe you are telling yourself to keep it together, suppress "it," hide "it," or don't talk about "it" too.

Well I believe that this moment with the pancakes was God's way of telling me that I needed to stop pretending. I believe He knew that the result of burying my pain was only going to trickle over and cause a bigger mess. But hey, I'm human, and just as a kid might not learn not to go near the stove until they're burned, I had to learn by experience. I also believe He wanted me to know that I was spending so much time and energy pretending for everyone else, when all He wanted me to do was cry out to Him and acknowledge that I wasn't okay. I didn't have to keep hiding what was really going on. I just choose to, and the fallout of that one choice was going to change the trajectory of my whole life. So, let's flash back to see where it all began.

2013

It was the summer before I left for college. I was so excited to leave home. I thought this is my new start, this is where I'm going to meet the man of my dreams, this is going to be my new home for the next four years. I was beyond ready to leave home and start my journey. I remember going in my living room at home at least twice a day and gloating as all my belongings began to pile up. It was getting real; my move-in date was quickly approaching. Each day I would walk into the living room with my checklist of items that I needed to bring. I would check that list once or twice just to make sure I wasn't forgetting any of the essentials.

Fast forward to move-in day, my parents and I loaded up the SUV and we made our way to the beautiful Shenandoah valley. About three hours later we arrived at my new home away from home and were greeted by some very enthusiastic and excited individuals dressed in bright yellow shirts and khaki shorts. Immediately they started grabbing things out of the car and taking them to my assigned dorm room. *This is great*, I thought. *This is my type of energy.* (If you know anything about me at all, I am a very friendly individual. Overly friendly, some may say.) Once everything was loaded into my dorm, we began to assemble the room. My dad worked on one thing, while my mom and I tackled another. My roommate hadn't arrived just yet, so I took first pick and grabbed the bed closest to the window and the AC. After we finished assembling everything, grabbed lunch, met my roommate and her family, we said our goodbyes. I hugged and kissed my parents and they were off. *I'm a whole adult. I'm free.*

The first week felt like summer camp. They called it "FROG" week at my school. It was the week that all the freshmen got acclimated to campus life, had a bunch of programs, etc. It was also the week that I attended my first college party. My roommate and I had already gotten to know a few upperclassmen at the university thanks to an Instagram page for incoming freshman, so we found ourselves with an invite to an off-campus party. We got dressed and found our way to the campus bus. Our next stop: Greenwood Apartments (not the real name).

I can't really remember exactly all the events of that night but all I know was that there were so many parties going on. People had their doors open and welcomed anyone in. I got to try "jungle juice" at one of the girl's houses that I had met, and bam, a few cups in, I was drunk. I felt so good. I was living my best life already and classes hadn't even started yet. I had no one to report to and no curfew; it was great.

As the night went on, I remember stumbling into one house and meeting a guy who I would eventually latch on to. I smiled from ear to ear after talking to him. We exchanged numbers after talking for a bit and then we eventually parted ways. The last campus bus was coming so I had to make sure I was on it and didn't get left. Again, I thought, this is great. I loved the hype. I loved the parties. I loved being drunk. I loved the freedom that I felt. Soon this became the lifestyle for me.

Classes started and they were going great, however, I found myself always ready for the weekend. I couldn't wait for the next turn up. It became a lifestyle. A pattern. Some days I wouldn't even wait for the weekend. A Monday night drink was just fine. I had no shame. As long as my grades were good, I was good.

My first spring break quickly approached. Instead of going home, some of my friends and I loaded up the car to drive to Maryland. We were going to support my school's men's basketball team in a CAA Tournament in Baltimore Maryland.

I screamed my lungs out for the team the night of the game. I yelled as the opposing team players' were at the free throw line, and I cheered until my voice was nearly gone. The game was so good, but they ended up losing by nine points, so they were knocked out of the tournament.

Bummed at the loss, we cleared out of the arena and then headed to our next stop. One of my friends had a cousin in Washington D.C., so we stayed at his house for the night rather than driving all the way back home. Once we got settled in, we started drinking. We drank all night long, or at least that's what it felt like. I remember blasting the music, playing beer pong and other drinking games, and just having a great time. But eventually everything became blurry. That's when everything changed for me. Something "fun," something

I grew accustomed to, something I enjoyed, led to one of the most traumatic experiences in my life. It's that ugly pancake that I was hiding: sexual assault.

I remember two things from that night. Walking up the stairs to use the bathroom and waking up to someone hovering over me. I had blacked out that night. For how long . . . I have no recollection. The events leading up to it . . . I have no recollection. What I do know is that it was something that I would not have wanted nor asked for.

Like I said, it was the ugly pancake that I was hiding. *Not me, no way. . . that couldn't have really happened.* I felt so much guilt. I felt shame. I felt disgust. I felt betrayed. I felt worthless. Nevertheless, I let it get swept under the rug as if it never occurred.

I buried those emotions along with the encounter, the friends, and that entire night. For a year or so, I had suppressed that experience thinking that it would mysteriously go away, and I'd never have any other recollection of it. Those friends left the University months after for different reasons so I figured it would never come up again. This was my first mistake.

Questions seized my mind. Not just for a moment or for hours but for days that turned into weeks then to months and years. The questions kept coming. *Why me? Why this? Where were my friends? Why didn't they intervene? Why didn't they care? Why didn't I stop drinking? Why would anyone do that? WHY?*

My emotions went from confusion to anger to self-blame to bitterness to more confusion. I struggled to make sense of it. I couldn't make sense of it, so I went right back to doing what I knew.

I drank, I partied, I ran to a guy for comfort. But this time it wasn't for fun, it was because I needed those things in order to "drown my sorrows" as people say. Anytime I was alone, the questions and the memories would pop up, so I did anything to avoid being alone. I faked it for so long. I pretended. I pretended that I was living the good life and enjoying my time in college. but that was so far from the truth. Deep down, I had a secret that was crippling the very life I was trying to live. I just couldn't bring myself to acknowledge it though, so I kept running. I ran to food, alcohol, a guy, sleep. I ran to anything that I thought could make it go away. I was not in a good place at all, but nonetheless, I kept it buried.

I know that not everyone reading may share my experience. Maybe you do, but if you don't, maybe you resonate with my attempts to bury any and everything that could possibly remind me of that night. Maybe you've buried some friendships. An absent mother or father. Some painful event.

I believe that we have all done it at some point in our lives. We have all ran to something or someone whether knowingly or unknowingly to suppress a painful memory. Maybe you ran to a person. Maybe drugs. Sex. Food. Netflix. The gym. Sleep. We all are pretty different, but just sit with that for a second. Whether it's physical, emotional, mental, spiritual pain, or a combination of them, what do you do or rather what have you done with it?

I have found that many of us run to these things in order to suppress our pain rather than addressing it. You just read that is what I did.

I grew up in church, but if I'm being real, God was the last person on my mind at the time. How could I turn to Him after I had spent the last five months or so living my best life? I didn't believe that I could run to God at that point in my life, so the drinking, the guy, and the parties were my only resort.

I buried those things and continued to carry around all of that dead weight on me day after day after day, until finally I couldn't carry it anymore. I lasted nine months and then I broke.

Now that I sit here and type that out, I don't believe that it is a coincidence that it took exactly nine months until I broke. The majority of the time, a baby spends nine months inside a mother's womb. Now, I know that this isn't a baby, but for the sake of my point, bear with me. The baby in this scenario is the dead weight. I was carrying around dead weight, allowing it to grow and get bigger and bigger as time progressed. The only difference is that it wasn't growing healthier, it was growing deadlier.

In nine months of carrying dead weight, I didn't even notice the impact that it had on my health, on my actions, on my relationships, and on my mind.

I did some things that I wasn't proud of in those nine months. There were some decisions made that could've taken others' lives and put me in jail. I made some premature attempts to take my life. I cut my hair. I hurt myself. I hurt others. I did some things that were not like me at all—all because I decided to carry something that I was never intended to carry in the first place.

The drinking no longer worked for me, the parties became dull and pointless, and the guy eventually made the decision to walk out of my life. Everything that sustained me fell through. The baby—the dead weight—was a detriment to me, so at nine months I broke. I birthed death. I birthed the idea that the only real option I had left was to take my life. *Surely that would make the pain go away,* I thought.

I was so hopeless; so empty, so broken, and I felt so far from God. I was living out the consequences of what I had buried months prior.

Maybe your pain has never driven you that far, to the point where you no longer feel your life is valuable. Maybe it has, but the point that I'm trying to make by sharing this with you is that suppressing this event and the pain associated with it caused a snowball effect in my life.

Something seemingly small and harmless turned into something huge and potentially disastrous, and it is very possible that the same could happen to you. It is possible that the pain you are choosing to suppress is secretly sabotaging you in ways that you may not even know or in ways that it shouldn't. And I am not sure where your pain may fall on a scale from mild to extreme, but in my case it was extreme. So extreme that it almost took me out.

So, I am here so that we can stop this thing in its tracks. I'm here to help you put a stop to the dead weight that you may be birthing at this very moment. I'm here to tell you that your life *is* valuable, your pain *is* real, but so is our God. But we will get to the later part in a few moments. Just in case you still aren't convinced that burying your pain is dangerous, let's go to the Bible. This is truth that I was not alert to when I was in the thick of it. I grew up in church, so I knew scripture, but at that time in my life, it was far from my mind.

What I realize today is that I had an adversary—Satan—that wanted to take me out. In 1 Peter 5:8 it says, "Be sober-minded; be watchful. Your adversary the devil prowls around like a roaring lion, seeking someone to devour." (ESV) Not only this, but the Bible also says that his goal is to steal, kill, or destroy us (John 10:10). So, when I say that suppressing your pain can give him the leverage he needs in order to achieve those goals, I hope you believe me.

He knows our weakest areas and he attacks them. Scripture says that he prowls like a lion. Lions, from my recollection, study their prey and wait for the right moment to attack. In the same way, Satan studies us. He sees our weakness. The things we desire, the things that we idolize, the things that we run to in times of pain and struggle . . . our sin. Those are our weaknesses and he will try his hardest to use them.

He used Judas' weakness of money to take him out *(found in John 12:5-6 and Mathew 26:14-15)*. He tried it with Jesus after Jesus hadn't eaten for 40 days and nights *(found in Matthew 4:1-11)*, and you just heard how he tried it with me. And while I know that these are only a few examples, there are plenty more throughout the Bible, my life, and probably yours as well.

Please listen to me when I say that the enemy wants to take you out. He wants you to continue to live in and sulk in your pain. He wants to drive you to the point of misery. To the point of hopelessness. And maybe even to the point where the only clear option you see is to end your life. But friends, you don't deserve any of that. It may be difficult to see now, but it's quite the opposite.

You deserve joy. You deserve peace. You deserve freedom. And that joy, peace, and freedom starts the moment you are willing to address the pain. The moment you stop hiding that burnt pancake is the moment where your freedom can begin.

Friends, I don't want Satan to have the upper hand in your life. I don't want you to feel bound to your pain any longer. And I really don't want you birthing something that you were never meant to birth in the first place. But in order for any of these things to happen, you must do some digging. You must heed the same advice that God gave me: address the pain. Satan didn't want me to address my pain and he doesn't want you to address yours either. But it is so important.

So, I ask you now: what is it that you have suppressed? Or what is it that you are currently burying?

I know you may not be ready to face whatever your "it" is, but I am challenging you and encouraging you right now to make it your standard to address and not suppress. I challenge you to care and tend to those painful things you are feeling or have felt.

I assure you, addressing your pain is the first step toward your freedom. It's not an easy one but it is one of the first steps that I had to take in my journey, and it's the first step in yours as well.

Now, I hope and pray that at this moment you feel persuaded to begin this journey. And even if you don't feel ready right at this moment, know that I am rooting for you and praying for it to come, but please keep reading. Maybe, just maybe, God will speak to you through something shared and move your heart to action.

This journey is going to require some digging. It is also going to require you to lean into that discomfort and pain and fight even when it's tempting to give up, but it will be so worth it. I promise.

Chapter 2

Naming the Pain

In 2015, God brought a lovely friend into my life who had absolutely no boundaries. I mean that in the best way possible. She was invested in my life and in our relationship to the point where she could tell whenever something was wrong. It annoyed me at first because I didn't understand why she cared so much. She would ask me question after question after question to try to help me process what was going on, but my response, answer after answer after answer: *I don't know.*

I honestly didn't know. I didn't know how to put a name on what I was feeling. It was a myriad of emotions that I couldn't describe or label. But thank God, me and my stubbornness didn't drive this amazing friend away. She is still in my life and still as annoying as ever and all up in my business! But we all need at least friend in our life like her—the friends that are constantly trying to hold you accountable. The friends that want you to be better. We need them.

One day, standing in the tiny kitchen of our two-bedroom apartment, I remember this friend challenging me. She told me that she didn't want to hear me say "I don't know" anymore. She didn't want to hear it in my vocabulary. I probably said something smart or snarky back to her because I didn't want to listen, but I tried my best to listen to her challenge. It didn't happen the next day or the day after. It took a while for me to follow her challenge, but eventually, I tried it. While I did not always succeed, her annoying challenge allowed me to look deeper, to reflect, and to practice what I want to call "naming it."

She was challenging me to name what I was feeling. She was asking me to do something that felt impossible at the time.

Have you ever been there or experienced that? Have you ever experienced a moment where you couldn't put words to your feelings? Maybe all you could do was cry. Maybe you became so angry that you just completely shut down. Or maybe you kept it simple and just left it at "I don't know" like me.

Wherever you find yourself, I now share with you the same challenge that my friend once shared with me, to try naming the pain you are feeling.

Maybe you already know what you are feeling? Maybe you find that you are experiencing a multitude of emotions that you don't know how to explain? Wherever you stand, I want you to try to name the pain.

2014

It's flashback time again, friends. This is a journey, so you are going to get all the juice from my journey just so you can see how I walked through the mud and mire.

As mentioned earlier, it wasn't until 2015 that this friend came into my life and challenged me to name the pain. God brought her into my life when I was broken and shattered and was attempting to piece my life back together, but the pain existed long before she came into my life, so we must go back in time.

Continuing from where I left off, the drinking was no longer working, the parties felt pointless, and the guy had decided to end things. Everything that I looked to for comfort was no longer an option. I felt so broken, so empty, so crushed. I just wanted the pain to end. I wanted to reverse time and stop the feelings and the thoughts. It hurt too much. It hurt too much to wake up every day and suddenly be drowned with the memories and thoughts. It was as if they were on replay and I couldn't stop them no matter how hard I tried. The only option I saw left was to take my life. I contemplated it. I really wanted to do it, but on the other hand I really didn't want to do it.

I was a sophomore in college at this time and I vividly remember sitting in corners in my bedroom or on my bathroom floors most days contemplating this option. *Should I do it? Should I not do it?*

I had moved into my first apartment, and it was a nice size four-bedroom apartment that I shared with two of my friends from freshman year. Each room had its own personal bathroom, so many days, I would lock myself in my room and not come out unless I had class. I remember days that I would even wait by my bedroom door to make sure no one was in the common area so I could make a mad dash for the front door without having to speak to anyone. Once I made it safely out of the apartment, I was good to go for the rest of the day. It was rare for me to run into people that I knew since my campus was so huge and my main classes were in the same building.

  I would go to class then go straight home and back to my room. No one ever really knew what went on behind those doors. No one knew how I suffered in silence, so ashamed of the feelings and thoughts I was having. Each night I would lay out a few comforters out on my bathroom floor so I would have some cushion while laying down, and that is where I resided most of the time. It was the only place I felt safe. It was the only place that no one could hear me. It was the only place I could sleep without hearing the laughing and conversations that taunted me. I slept on that bathroom floor.

  Thoughts ran through my mind constantly wondering what other people's life would be like without me, though I was convinced that it wouldn't really matter whether or not I was alive. I had no interest in being around people or interest in life in general. I was always exhausted and slept a lot. Eventually I became numb. I went through my daily routines but didn't feel like I was actually present. I desperately needed help, but I dared not tell anyone that I was experiencing any of these feelings. I was drowning. Alone.

  Some nights, if I got tired of sitting in the bathroom, I would hop in the car and just drive. I guess I thought that I could drive the pain away. I thought that maybe, just maybe if I drove long enough, I'd reach a destination where I could just lay it all down and return to my normal life. And if that didn't work, maybe a deer would jump out and wreck my car. Or maybe I could drive into a ditch. Nothing that I did could shake the dark cloud hovering over me. No friend, no man, no drink, no drive, no sex, no food, nothing.

I never shared with anyone in my life how I was truly feeling at that time. Of course, God knew because I spent hours crying out to Him but that was it. I couldn't let people know that I wasn't put together. After all, I claimed to be a Christian and Christians are supposed to be grateful for life, not wanting to end their life. Right? *Wrong.*

I was conflicted. I couldn't understand why I couldn't seem to be grateful for a life that I was so fortunate to have. I would sit there and rehearse all that I had to be grateful for. *I have two amazing parents who love and care for me. They support me. I have a brother who cares for me. I had a pretty great upbringing. I'm fortunate to be able to go to college. I'm fortunate to have clothes on my back and food in my kitchen. I'm fortunate to be able to wake up each and every day.* The list went on. But as the list grew, so did the guilt and shame that told me to just keep how I was feeling to myself, and so I did.

This went on for months. All these emotions were bottled up with a tight corkscrew to keep them tucked away. It was like this gross cocktail of pain, shame, guilt, anger, bitterness, sadness, fear, rejection, and anxiety bottled up together; it wasn't pretty at all. I don't know if you ever use to play with condiments as a child, but I remember combining things like ketchup, ranch dressing, soy sauce, barbeque sauce, and whatever else I could get my hands on. I would create my own concoction.

As you can imagine, that is a pretty gross combination. And while all those emotions that I had bottled up didn't create something physically distasteful, they produced something mentally distasteful. They produced a feeling I couldn't describe.

Eventually, over the months, I couldn't distinguish one emotion from another. I no longer knew how to accurately put words to all that I felt. I couldn't describe it or explain it, so I stopped trying.

It wasn't until years later, when I actually addressed that something was wrong, that I was able to put a name on the feeling. It wasn't until years later that I was able to name the pain. Do you want to know what I named it?

I named it *darkness*.

Darkness

Darkness.

As I thought about these feelings that I couldn't really put into words or describe, the word darkness came to mind. This was the name I gave to the messy concoction of emotions that I had going on internally.

This darkness made me feel like a giant school bus just plopped down on top of me, without the wheels, pinning me to the cement. It made me feel like a snake was tightly coiled around my body leaving me gasping for simply a tiny bit of air. It felt like this weight inside my body that no amount of deep breathing, stretching, shaking, or moving could erase. I had no control. It left me feeling powerless. Hopeless. Exhausted. Anxious. Worried. It caused tears at random moments. It left me lost for words. This was my darkness.

Now I am going to tread very lightly here because what this book is NOT is a diagnostic tool. These are simply my experiences and my thoughts. But, for me, this darkness seemed pretty similar to that "d" word that many people are afraid to use. Depression. This is what I felt. This is what I feel sometimes. This is my darkness.

And while I know that much of what I shared is heavy, I promised to give you the raw truth, so that's it. I struggled. I still struggle. This darkness is an ugly thing.

Satan wanted me to believe that I was alone. That I was the only one, and maybe I was at that time, but chances are I wasn't. Chances are, there were many people suffering around me. Chances are, there are many people suffering in silence, victim to Satan's lies, and being choked by the darkness they feel even at this very moment. Chances are, that very person could be you or someone you know.

But I have good news for you. The Bible says in John 1:5, "The light shines in the darkness, and the darkness has not overcome it." The light that they are referring to here is Jesus. Darkness has not overcome Him, *present tense*.

When I thought about this, I thought about all the forms of light that we have, both natural and man-made. The sun, the moon, nightlights, flashlights, headlights. They all have the same purpose; they help us find our way when it's dark outside.

This one night I was in my apartment alone, and it was a rough night. It was a night that I had spent crying my eyes out for reasons that I can't remember at this moment, but the second that I turned off all the lights in the place, my room was illuminated. Not by my iPhone's flashlight or the colored light from my alarm clock that I never use. It was light from my window. I went to peak outside and just above my apartment was a beautiful full moon. A full moon that reminded me that no matter what darkness I feel, the light will still shine. It will always shine.

We all need that reminder. We all need the reminder that the light (Jesus) shines in darkness and He has not been overcome. No matter what is going on in our life, God is and will always be on the throne. But that's not the main point that I am trying to make here, though it is a good point.

The point here is that Satan wants us to think that we are alone in our struggles in life. That it is a *me* thing not a *them* thing. He wants to convince us that we are on an island of one. That is so far from the truth.

Two of my favorite people ever in the Bible also felt this darkness: The prophet Jeremiah and King David who inspired the name of this book. Jeremiah was called to speak to God's people and oftentimes he brought a word that no one wanted to hear. While false prophets spoke comforting messages, Jeremiah brought truth. And because this was the life that he was called to live, he grew disheartened. (Jeremiah 20 NIV) Jeremiah said "cursed be the day that I was born." (vs. 14) In other words, he was wishing that he was never born. He suffered much of his life feeling lonely and defeated because no one would listen. That's a rough life to have to live, if you ask me.

Similarly, David struggled with darkness of his own. If you read through some of his Psalms and 2 Samuel, you will learn that he was in a position where he was being pursued constantly by his enemies. People were out to get him for different reasons. Not only this, but his own son tried to kill him, he suffered through the loss of one of his close friends, and he lost his baby boy. I can understand why David found himself stuck in this deep pit too.

And while I briefly pointed these out to show that we are often not alone, I also found that both of these men went to the Lord in prayer and named it. Both David and Jeremiah go to the Lord and name their pain. In Psalm 42, David names what he is feeling as downcast. In Jeremiah 20, Jeremiah names what he is feeling also. He feels deceived, hoodwinked, bamboozled. They put a name to their feelings. I put a name to my feelings. Now, you must put a name to your feelings as well. Don't complain or groan. There is probably something, some kind of thorn or issue in your life that is crippling you in ways that you wish it wouldn't. It may be rejection, shame, insecurity, or darkness. But something in your life needs to be named, so it's your turn. Name it.

Maybe it's darkness you are feeling too. Maybe it's shame. Betrayal. Rejection. Bitterness. Anger. Maybe there is some combination of what you are feeling.

I'm not going to sugar coat this. You need to put a name on your feelings. It's so important to put a name to your feeling. So important. Must I say it again? Friends, I know that there's a thing that is tormenting you or maybe someone in close proximity to you. Perhaps a friend, a parent, a cousin, a classmate. I know that there is some pain, some feeling, something that needs to go—to flee.

Don't be like me and keep saying that you don't know what you are feeling. Don't settle with not knowing or not being willing to explore it. Examine your life so you can name the pain. *Please.*

I'm just going to go out on a limb and assume you agreed to examine your life. However, I haven't told you why you need to examine your life or shown you why it is so important. So maybe I should do that. There are two reasons that I say this and why I dedicated this entire chapter to naming your pain.

Reason One

One reason is that "naming it" gives you power over it. The best example I can give you of this is through Jesus. The Lord placed Matthew 4 on my mind and I read it three times, and what I found is pretty interesting. First, let's look at the text.

> Then Jesus was led up by the Spirit into the wilderness to be tempted by the devil. And when He had fasted forty days and forty nights, afterward He was hungry. Now when the tempter came to Him, he said, "If You are the Son of God, command that these stones become bread." But He answered and said, "It is written, 'Man shall not live by bread alone, but by every word that proceeds from the mouth of God.' "Then the devil took Him up into the holy city, set Him on the pinnacle of the temple, and said to Him, "If You are the Son of God, throw Yourself down. For it is written: 'He shall give His angels charge over you,' and, 'In *their* hands they shall bear you up, Lest you dash your foot against a stone.' "Jesus said to him, "It is written again, 'You shall not tempt the Lord your God.' "Again, the devil took Him up on an exceedingly high mountain, and showed Him all the kingdoms of the world and their glory. And he said to Him, "All these things I will give You if You will fall down and worship

me." Then Jesus said to him, "Away with you, Satan! For it is written, 'You shall worship the Lord your God, and Him only you shall serve.'" Then the devil left Him, and behold, angels came and ministered to Him" (Matthew 4:1-11).

    I wonder if you caught it when you read it. What I noticed is that it wasn't until the third time, the time that Jesus called it by its name "Satan," that he fled. Now I don't know if Jesus knew that it was Satan all along or what Jesus was thinking at that moment. If I was him, I probably would've tried to push him off the cliff and go get some food. After all, I had just finished forty days of fasting and now this tempter wants to come bother me.

    Did I take it too far? I would never actually push anyone off a cliff, I promise. But, I have no sympathy for Satan. The relevant matter is that in verse 10, Jesus says, "Away with you, Satan," and in verse 11, it says, "then the devil left him."

    When Jesus spoke and called the tempter by his true name, it caused him to flee. This is what the Lord revealed to me. Friends, giving a name to your feelings gives you a power over them that you wouldn't otherwise have.

Reason Two

    The second reason is that until you can name it, you don't even know what you are fighting against. The enemy is very clever in how he attacks us, but if we never know what he is attacking, how can we really combat the attack? Would you fight the flu with tums? Chances are you probably wouldn't, but if you didn't know that it was the flu you were fighting, then what?

That may not have been the best example, so think of it like this. In the field of Mental Health, there is this book called the *DSM-5* or the *Diagnostic and Statistical Manual of Mental Disorders*, that is used by psychiatrists, psychologists, counselors, and other health professionals. It is a comprehensive guide that clinicians use to diagnose mental disorders. Things like depression, PTSD, OCD, and agoraphobia, are a few of the maladies discussed, but there are hundreds of disorders listed. (I only know because as I am writing this chapter, I am currently in a class and this is my textbook. Imagine having to read through it though; it's intense.)

The DSM has been around for years, but over time it still has the same purpose: to help diagnose mental disorders. This is not to put a label on someone or to outcast them, but to take the first step in helping people get better. Thousands of researchers, clinicians, and health professionals from various disciplines have gotten together for years and created this manual, updating and revising it, to help people get better. But if a diagnosis was never given, how could it be treated? In the same manor, if we never name our pain, how would we know how to heal from it? We wouldn't because you can't treat what you don't know.

Let me be clear, I am not telling you to go buy the DSM-5 and try to diagnose yourself. I do not recommend that at all. I am simply using that as an example to show you that it is critical to do some soul searching in order to know what is beneath the surface in order to begin this journey.

Final Thoughts

As I laid in the dark one night around 8 pm, my mind was racing, and my heart was beating so fast that I just wanted to force myself to sleep. I laid there waiting and wanting it to stop. Without even thinking about it, I started ranting. I told God that I wanted the darkness to stop. It was that moment, without even realizing it, that I named it.

While it did not flee immediately like Satan did when Jesus named it, in the days and months that followed, the power that I once felt stripped of began to come back to me. The darkness slowly, very slowly, but surely, began to flee, all because I made the decision to name it. But that wasn't all I had to do. You have to keep reading to see what was next.

Chapter 3

Sitting in Darkness

Well friends, you kept reading. *Whoop, whoop!* In chapter one, I encouraged you to address the pain that you may have suppressed or are currently trying to suppress. We also talked about how the enemy can and will use our pain against us if we let him. In chapter two, we talked about naming the pain. Now, we must move forward, but in order to do that I think it's imperative that we talk about our mindset. I was originally going to get rid of this chapter but after some deliberation with God, I think that He wants me to keep it.

So, our mindset. I've realized that a lot of times I say I want something, but my actions say otherwise. It's similar to when you want to start eating healthier, but those salted potato chips and sugary treats keep calling your name, so you give in once. Before you know it, your whole "healthy lifestyle" plan is out the window. Or is it just me?

Well, it's kind of the same with this. There are so many things that can stand in your way as you try to be healthier spiritually, mentally, and emotionally. Especially if it seems like you've been dealing with the same thing for what feels like years now. But in order to rise from the miry clay, we can't stay there. And that has a lot to do with the mindset that we choose to approach this thing with.

There are mindsets that have got to go.

Mind Reading

Would you believe me if I told you that I could read your mind? You probably wouldn't because I can't. But I like to think I can sometimes.

When I considered my own thoughts during my journey, I realized that I often fell guilty to mind reading, leaving me in silence. I often assumed how people would react or respond though I had little evidence to suggest that may have been the case. Silly as it sounds, I was trying to read minds.

According to cogbtherapy.com, *cognitive distortions* are defined as errors or biases in thinking that can lead to faulty assumptions and can worsen a mood. One common cognitive distortion is mind reading, which is assuming you know what other people think though there may not be evidence to suggest its truth.

Now I am no neuropsychologist, but I am seriously intrigued by the brain. I find it extremely interesting that certain experiences and circumstances that we go through can shape our lens of how we look at people and events. One action by a person can destroy how we view every single person in our life. One event or one experience can lead to cognitive distortions like mind reading.

So, because my curiosity was piqued, I conducted a little research experiment of my own. I grabbed my phone and reached out to different men and women in my life and I asked what keeps them from sharing or opening up about anything in their lives. I reached out to at least thirteen or fourteen people. I was hoping that they would confirm that I was not alone in this thinking. I wasn't! Five of ten of the most common reasons dealt with assumptions of how other people would react or respond. They dealt with mind reading.

Common responses were:
1. "I'll be a burden."
2. "People won't care."
3. "People won't understand."
4. "People need me to be strong for them."
5. "People will minimize it."

So, where do these beliefs come from exactly? That is a great question! I am convinced that as I said before, events or situations that we have experienced in our life may have altered our desire to ask for or accept help. We may have experienced a reaction in times that we decided to open up and share, and the reaction received was one that left a bad taste. Or maybe we have witnessed someone else in our life opening up only to be shut down? In either case, these experiences can often lead us to draw assumptions about how other people will react. And to be honest, sometimes we will get reactions that leave a bitter taste in our mouth, but I come to challenge you to keep an open mindset despite those moments.

I say this because one thing I have realized and am currently working on is not labeling other people based off of one person's reactions. This is exactly what mind reading is and what mind reading does. I have pushed away many people in my life because I assumed that they would react the same way that someone in my past did. And that is not fair to people in our lives, nor is it fair to ourselves. I sat in darkness void of many people to turn to because I assumed that I would get shut out or shut down. I figured that I was protecting myself, but it was only making me feel more miserable. Those mind reading tendencies kept me in a place of darkness fighting alone.

And while I am not face to face with you to ask you personally if you recognize the same tendencies in your life, if you do see these tendencies, I challenge you to explore them.

This book is about exploration and this chapter specifically is about weeding out the lies that we may believe. Lies that keep us in a place of dormancy. It is simply not enough to read these words. If you find yourself rejecting help or refusing to ask for help because you hold beliefs that you are a burden or that people won't care, or any other reason that you find, I challenge you to explore it. Explore your upbringing and your life up to this point and try to find where this belief may have been planted. Ask God to reveal to you the moments in your life where you may have latched on to these beliefs.

Ask yourself questions like:
- Why do I believe that this is true?
- Is this a pattern I have seen in my past that I am projecting onto this person?
- Is there evidence to suggest it is truth or am I assuming?

I hope you find these questions to be useful as you navigate your mind reading tendencies.

Maybe mind reading didn't really speak to you, well maybe this next section will.

Pride

Brace yourself for this next one. No one likes to be told that they are being prideful. In fact, I remember the first time someone told me that I was acting in pride. I immediately became defensive and thought, *No I'm not,* as if that statement of denial wasn't enough proof. But, the truth is pride can come in a whole variety of shapes, expressions, and forms. Some that we often don't recognize or may not consider pride.

I wrote a little about the responses that fell under the mind reading tendencies, so now let me point out the responses I received that may fall under the pride category:
1. "I'm strong enough."
2. "I can't show weakness or vulnerability."
3. "I'm ashamed/embarrassed."

I want to break down each of these and show you how it can be considered pride.

"I'm strong enough" is a response that many people shared with me and one that I identified with as well. And while I hate to be the bearer of bad news, this kind of thinking has pride written all over it. You may be asking yourself why. Well, the belief that you are strong enough to handle your own problems claims self-sufficiency.

Maybe you haven't necessarily believed that you are strong enough, but you have used the words,

"I've got this," to give yourself a small pep talk. Well, I'd like to suggest that if you consider yourself to be Christian, you may want to remove this simple but harmful statement from your vocabulary. John 15:5 states, "I am the vine; you are the branches. If you remain in me and I in you, you will bear much fruit; apart from me you can do nothing." That last part of the verse is what is important here. Jesus is telling the disciples that apart from Him they can do nothing. This same principle applies to us.

In a society that is ever increasing in independence and self-reliance, I would like to suggest that falling into this pattern will lead to destruction. **You cannot overcome darkness on your own.** You cannot overcome your problems in life alone, and contrary to what you may believe, you are not strong enough.

I learned this harsh truth through the Lord's prophet, Elijah. We find in 1 Kings 18, Elijah trying to defend and prove that he is the Lord's prophet. At that time, the people were listening to the false prophets of Baal, but Elijah was sent to tell them about themselves and how they were wrong. Well, things go awry, and Elijah ends up running from Ahab and his wife Jezebel. Elijah had killed the prophets, so Jezebel sent a message to Elijah: "You killed my prophets. Now I'm going to kill you..." (1 Kings 19:2). The text goes on to say, "Elijah was afraid when he got her message, and he ran to the town of Beersheba in Judah" (vs. 3).

If we go back to 1 Kings 18, we see that after Elijah killed the prophets of Baal, the Lord gave him strength to go to Jezreel (vs. 46). However, in 1 Kings 19, we see that Elijah became afraid when he received word that Jezebel was going to kill him, so he ran to Beersheba (vs. 3).

The Lord supplied Elijah with the strength to get where he needed to go (Jezreel). BUT the moment that Elijah became afraid, he started relying on his own strength and ran to a place that he was NOT instructed to go (Beersheba). Eventually, he gets tired on his journey and asks the Lord to let him die there (1 Kings: 19:4). And while the Lord does not grant Elijah's request, I'd like to suggest that had Elijah not called out to the Lord, he too, would have remained in a dark place trying to figure it out on his own. Wishing that he was dead. But in his cry of desperation, the Lord provided him food and drink in order to give him strength yet again for his journey.

Relying on his own strength left him in a place where he dreaded his own life. And though I do not know the totality of what Elijah may have been experiencing in those moments, I hope this example gives you just a small glimpse of how and why relying on your own strength or believing that "you got this," can actually lead to destruction. There is only fruit and life when we abide in the Lord. Apart from Him, we truly cannot do anything (John 15:5).

"I can't show weakness or vulnerability" was another response that I received from people and one I believed myself. What I have found about this statement is that it can be tied to perfectionism or people pleasing, amongst many other things. While I will not go into detail, I would like to debunk this statement by showing you how weakness is actually a great thing.

The apostle Paul is a great example to write about here. In 2 Corinthians 12:9-10, Paul states, "but he said to me, "My grace is sufficient for you, for my power is made perfect in weakness." Therefore I will boast all the more gladly about my weaknesses, so that

Christ's power may rest on me. That is why, for Christ's sake, I delight in weaknesses, in insults, in hardships, in persecutions, in difficulties. For when I am weak, then I am strong."

Paul recognized that no matter what he was facing, no matter how bad the trial, storm, or persecution was, it was an opportunity for God's strength to shine through. The suffering that Paul had endured in his lifetime was severe but no matter what, he was able to rejoice. He chose to rejoice. **He chose to brag about his weakness because bragging about his weakness also gave him the opportunity to brag about Jesus.**

When we are afraid or unwilling to admit weakness, we stifle what can be done through us. We stifle the ability for God to move through and in us and in others. You see, our weakness sets an example to those around us.

You know, sitting here thinking about it, I think that this is a reason that many people get a false sense of what it means to be Christian. There is this false idea circulating in the world that being Christian exempts us from life's problems, but it is actually the opposite. We are actually qualified to endure storms because we claim to be Christ followers, and when we show perfection or are afraid to show that we, too, experience weakness, this can confuse people and lead to this false idea.

Paul tells the Philippians that it is an immense privilege to suffer for Christ (Philippians 1:29). Isn't that crazy? That in his weakness, in his suffering, in his life, Paul was able to rejoice and boast because he saw his situation to be a privilege to have?

This truly convicted me when I read it. I was sitting at my dining table one day playing music and trying to spend time with God, but it felt like nothing was sticking. I felt empty. I felt like I was struggling but I downplayed it. I was supposed to go to a festival with a friend that I hadn't hung out with in a while and I really didn't want to go. I tried to convince myself that going was going to be good for me, but I ended up telling her that I wasn't okay. You see, I was going to do it again. I was going to pretend and show that I was good rather than admitting that I wasn't okay. That I was struggling and feeling extremely weak, exhausted, and depleted. I picked up my phone and texted her telling her exactly how I was feeling, and her response was:

"Brittany it's okay . . . I'll be praying over you, stay encouraged. It's a privilege to suffer in Christ. 'For it has been granted to you on behalf of Christ not only to believe in him, but also to suffer for him,' Philippians 1:29. Crazy to count suffering at all a privilege but it is in Christ because we know the power that comes with being a believer."

Little does she know, but this text sent me into a day of exploring Paul's life and learning about suffering. I was not only thrown off by her words, but I was also extremely encouraged. *Okay so, weakness is good. Suffering is good. Got it.*

I literally studied all of Paul's letters where he discussed being a prisoner for Christ and suffering. I finally understood that I could choose to rejoice in my suffering. I could embrace weakness even though it didn't necessarily feel good to show or be weak.

Prior to her encouragement, I would skip church because I knew that I would be a wreck. That, or I would sit in the back corner instead of my normal spot in the first or second row at church, so no one would come over and speak to me or notice me. I was trying to hide what God wanted me to embrace. I was taking for granted the ability to suffer for Christ.

Suffering for Christ is an amazing privilege that you and I have. Showing weakness may not feel the best. It may not feel good at all. In fact, it may leave you open, exposed, and vulnerable. **But it is when we are able to embrace our weak moments that God can use us.** It is in these weak moments that others are able to see Him. Because when you are weak and unafraid to show that, it pushes you to keep on pressing on. It pushes you to put one foot in front of the other and to continue marching towards Christ and out of that darkness.

And I realize that this may sound like a contradiction because I am showing you how the Bible says that suffering is good, yet this book is about getting out of muddy and dark places. However, I hope to show you that getting out of the mud and mire is truly about growth and being transformed into the likeness of Christ. While I have wished and prayed away the darkness many times, God has shown me that despair is a mindset to transcend, and that sitting in mud and mire is all about how you view it.

Similar to the claim, "I can't show weakness," **"I'm ashamed/embarrassed"** can be tied to perfectionism or people pleasing, amongst many other things as well.

For a long time, I was embarrassed with the way I was feeling. *I'm not supposed to be depressed. I'm supposed to be living my best life and enjoying my twenties. I can't be depressed.* No. I struggled and embarrassment ate away at my core. It kept me silent. It kept me in those dark spaces. I felt like admitting how I was feeling made it real. I felt shame because I felt like I shouldn't have let it get that bad. I couldn't believe that I had let myself get to a breaking point.

For me, this all stemmed from the need to be or appear perfect. Sure, it may sound silly, but perfectionism is just as real as any disease. It picks apart everything that you do and makes you feel awful when you fall short.

But the truth is that while the Bible does instruct us to be like Christ and to be holy like Him (1 Peter 1:15), perfection is a quality that we will never be able to achieve in and of ourselves because of sin. Because of sin, we all fall short (Romans 3:23). Thus, I believe that this instruction was given in order to remind us that though we cannot achieve perfection by ourselves, we should always strive and make it our standard to be as Christlike as possible.

But, if being like Christ is our standard, why are we so ashamed of others' perception of us? Jesus was publicly humiliated. People watched Him carry a cross. People watched Him get beat. People watched Him die. Yet, we are ashamed or embarrassed when we can't get it together and stop crying. Or when we can't seem to get our life together. Let me just say, I am not here to condemn you. In fact, I'm really talking to myself right here; you are just reading the inner dialogue I am having with myself.

I sulked in shame and embarrassment because of what I believed other people were thinking. (There's that mind reading again.) And many of us do this same thing, though we may not realize it. Our shame and embarrassment may be tied directly to others. Desiringgod.com says, "When pride lives in our hearts, we're far more concerned with others' perceptions of us than the reality of our hearts."

May I suggest to you that you should only be concerned with Jesus' perception of you. Jesus and Jesus alone. What the next person is doing, saying, or thinking is not your business nor your concern. In fact, you don't know what they may or may not be saying, thinking, or doing (talking to myself again), but nonetheless, we must free ourselves from the shame and embarrassment that cripples us and keeps us struggling alone. **Shame is not from the Lord and neither is embarrassment.**

And as a side note, I'd also like to suggest that if you have people in your life that make you feel like you have to be perfect or people who shame you and make you feel embarrassed … maybe it's time to re-evaluate their significance in your life.

The last mindset is a universal one. It's not one to get rid of but one to embrace. It's one that everybody should know and remember.

Acceptance

Okay. I'll keep it short and sweet, but I need you to read these next statements very carefully and slowly. Deal? I need you to process them. Okay, here it goes. It is okay to admit that you are not okay.

There, I said it. I said what everyone needs to hear and accept. Everyone needs to accept that it is okay to admit that you are not okay.

I saved the best for last. Let me tell you why. Our society and today's standards consistently tell us otherwise. They tell us to "keep it together," "fake it until you make it," "don't show weakness," "be strong," "don't talk about that in public." And while I'm sure that not everyone's intentions for saying these things are bad, they do leave an imprint on us. They cause us to internalize that "keeping it together" is the standard. However, **I am telling you right now that in order to experience true freedom, true peace and true joy, you need to accept that it is okay not to be okay.**

I remember sneaking into the back of church one morning hoping that no one would see me walk in. I usually sit in the first or second row. I like to be up close because not many people like to sit that far up, so it gives me space to worship. Also, I am easily distracted, so I don't want to be distracted by every single movement.

I thought I was doing a good job of sneaking in, but of course, one of my friends from the worship team saw me and waved from on stage. I waved reluctantly and made my way to a seat. I didn't sit in the far back but like midway; that way I would blend in a bit. Well, that didn't work either.

I didn't want people to see me because I wasn't okay. It took everything in me to get up, get dressed, and drive to church. I didn't want to be there, and I didn't want anyone knowing what was going on with me at the time.

As I stood there worshipping, I just broke. It was a combination of the words they were singing and the Lord stirring my heart. I wanted to run out of the sanctuary, but I couldn't. I couldn't move my feet. I just stood there and cried. After the worship set was over, I still cried. I couldn't stop. One of the guys from the worship team was walking by and he placed his hand on my back and it was as if he was acknowledging my hurt. Without words, I heard his assurance that it was okay to feel the way I was feeling. Moments later another friend came, and she just hugged me. I sat there in the middle of service so ashamed that I couldn't keep it together, but she just held me and let me know that it was okay.

I wanted to keep it together. I didn't want everyone to see me like that. I was struggling with the stigma and with pride. I was struggling to accept that it was okay not to be okay.

But the thing that I didn't know then that I recognize now, is that the church is the one place where I can be broken—the one place I should be comfortable not keeping it together. Church is not for perfect people but for broken people. And we all are pretty broken if you ask me. But again, that is okay.

You. Me. Your best friend. The woman who leads all the Bible studies. The man who kills every workout. The person that gets an "A" on every test. The most well-spoken pastor. Yes, we are all broken.

To Sum it Up

I have shared several reasons, statements, or mindsets that can potentially keep us in a space of darkness. These are common responses that myself and other people in my life have shared. Now, please hear me when I say that these are not ALL of the things that can essentially keep you in a place of darkness. These are things that I have found that do from personal experience and from shared experiences. You may find another reason specifically that keeps you in that place. And if you do, I'm still going to challenge you to explore. I challenge you to push through these feelings or views that you have regarding your struggles and what other people may think about them. It's going to be uncomfortable, but it's going to be good for you. I guarantee it.

I was reading an article called "Sit with it: A new way to work with depression" and I love what the author Erin Telford wrote. She says, "Depression is an opportunity for internal exploration. You are not depressed because you are a bad person or you skipped too many days of yoga or gratitude journaling. You are depressed because something is not working for you. There is a yearning. An emotional chasm. Something that is crying out to be witnessed and seen like it's never been seen before." It is my hope that in the next few chapters, you will see how true her words are. That your bitterness is an opportunity for internal exploration. Your shame, guilt, anxiety, and regret is an opportunity for internal exploration. That darkness, depression, or whatever pain you are experiencing is an opportunity for internal exploration. Internal exploration with God, that is.

PART 2

Waiting on God
Actively Uncovering the Pain

I waited patiently for the Lord;
he turned to me and heard my cry.
Psalm 40:1 NIV

Chapter 4

Get Up Child

As I ended the previous chapter, I said that this was going to be an opportunity for internal exploration with God. But before we get there, I just want to briefly review what we've learned so far.

We've talked about certain toxic mindsets that we will not let hinder us in this journey. We've also talked about addressing our pain by acknowledging that something is not right and naming our pain.

So, now we get into the action phase. And I just want to mention that I'm not endorsing that this is a perfect formula or an order that will ensure your ultimate healing, but it is what has worked for me and what I believe that God wants me to share with you. The next step is to get up. This may seem simple but is not really that simple at all.

I personally believe that getting up is always one of the toughest things to do in dark times. You want to get up, you want to make a change, and you want to be better, but better seems to be so far from your reach at times, and healing sometimes seems impossible.

How do you convince yourself to get up when it feels like everything around you is crumbling? When life is moving at a million miles per hour and you just can't hold on. When you are questioning your entire existence. How do you get up when the voices in your head keep screaming at you telling you that you don't matter and you are meaningless, useless, purposeless? How do you get up when you feel like a complete and utter failure? Like you can't get anything right or when you're in so much pain that it just seems easier to give up than to keep trying. How do you get up?

If you asked me any of these questions in 2015, I might have told you that I didn't know. I would've told you to please enlighten me, because for a long time I didn't know, but I was desperately searching for the answers. I wanted to be free. I wanted to stop the dark, gory thoughts. I wanted life to stop moving so fast. I wanted to feel meaningful, useful, and purposeful. I wanted to feel good and be happy. I wanted to be free from all the emotions, pain, and darkness. But it was just a foreign feeling to be "free" from the pain. I suffered in pain for so long that I didn't know anything but pain. We danced, we sang, we ate, we cried, and we lived together for so long it that pain became my best friend. And I couldn't see past it. I couldn't see past her. She disguised herself as someone that was here to stay. She bamboozled me. She tricked me into believing that this was my new life and that I just had to accept it. So, I did. Freedom became accepting things for what they were. Accepting my new life living with pain.

I kept saying that I wanted to be healed. I kept saying that I wanted change. But what God eventually showed me was that I said I wanted those things, but I was doing nothing to get there. I was doing nothing that would push me closer to any of those things. I was doing nothing that would push me closer to healing. And, so, there was a point, multiple points actually, that God prompted me to "get up." And that nudge of encouragement from God is exactly what I am going to share with you in this chapter, my friends.

So, when you think about getting up, what do you imagine? What comes to your mind? For me, I picture myself getting up from a nap or getting up from the couch. Or maybe a mom in a grocery story telling her toddler to get up off the floor while having a temper tantrum.

There are endless possibilities of what those words may mean to you, but I have found that many times people associate them with punishment or yelling or fussing. That's the first thing one of my friends mentioned when I asked her. She associated the phrase "get up" with her mother's scolding for her to get up for church on Sundays growing up. Similarly, I associated "get up" with punishment. But what I had to realize is that when God told me to "get up," He wasn't yelling at me. He was encouraging me. He was encouraging me to get up both physically and mentally. His prompting was to stop sitting around and wallowing in pity and pain and actually do something about it. I believe that He was telling me to be proactive in the midst of my pain.

And let me tell you, it's all how you interpret and read those words. I can see how the words "get up" can be interpreted falsely. They can be interpreted in a way that makes it seem like it's not okay to be down or to be struggling and weak. But that is not what God was telling me at all. He wanted my freedom more than I wanted it, and He knew that what I was doing and how I was living wouldn't get me there. And the same may be the case for you, so I want to take a moment and share God's heart for you. To do this we are going to take a few moments and practice guided imagery. I would suggest that you read first and then engage.

    I want you to imagine yourself in a dark moment. Maybe you were in bed crying yourself to sleep. Maybe you were sitting in your tub. Maybe you are sitting on your couch in the dark with your cup of alcohol in hand. Maybe you are laying on the floor. Maybe you are sitting in your parked car in the quiet garage. Wherever it may be, imagine yourself in that place where you feel the darkness and loneliness. Feel the emotions that you felt or are currently feeling. Allow yourself to really feel the weight of the pain. Allow yourself to feel the weight of every emotion that comes up. The hurt, the anger, the rejection, the betrayal. Feel those emotions. Now imagine this person, this figure, coming into the dark space. His walk is graceful. His presence creates this light. Can you see him walking? Take a deep breath.

    Now, imagine that this person is God. God is walking over to you. He kneels down and begins to talk to you. He is speaking so softly, so real, that you can almost hear the pain in His voice from seeing you hurt. Imagine Him telling you, get up daughter. Get up son. It's almost as if He is pleading and begging you to get up. Pleading and begging you not to give up on yourself. Pleading that you would not give up on life.

Take a second and sit with that. Sit with the thought of God, the creator of the universe, the creator of everything we see every day of our lives, kneeling down to plead with you, to be with you in your darkness. Imagine Him meeting you right there in the midst of your pain. Just sit with Him for a second. Now take a few moments and take some deep breaths. In through your nose, out through your mouth. In through your nose, out through your mouth. Once you are ready, come back to this space. Take another deep breath.

I hope and pray that that was as therapeutic for you as it was for me as I was typing it out. It is powerful when you are able to invite God into your darkness. It is powerful and comforting when you allow Him to whisper sweet encouragement to you.

He is not absent. He has not given up on you or turned away like the voice in our head sometimes tries to tell us. No. He is with you now and forever.

2014

In 2014, God reminded me that He was present even though I was convinced otherwise. As you may recall from previous chapters, my bathroom was my hiding place for some time. That is where I grew comfortable and could scream, cry, yell, or whatever else I needed to do. Well, there was one day I remember so vividly now, that I stared at the knife that I had with me in my bathroom. I'm sure you can guess what I wanted to do with it. But this is one of the moments I felt the Lord's prompting to get up. This is one of the moments where His grace met me.

God told me to look in the mirror and He reminded me of my worth. Now I was nowhere near my phone or anything but an event at my local church called "the Engine" came to mind. It was only God's doing. The Engine was a Friday night service that was a time of empowerment. There was a message, a time for prayer, and a time for prophecy. It was Friday, so I hopped in the car and made my way to church.

I remember sitting in that second row and I just felt numb. I heard the message, I loved the worship set, but it didn't feel like anything had changed. We went into a time of prayer during the event and I don't remember the exact words, but I just remember one of the pastors saying that he felt that there were people in the room needing something and so he encouraged us to pray for that specific thing. People who had a prophetic gift began to walk around and prophesy. As I sat there in that moment, I remember telling God that I was feeling worthless and just wanted to take my life. I was maybe 19 or 20 years old at the time and I was tired of fighting. I told Him that I didn't feel like He was with me or that He even cared. I asked Him why I had to be sexually assaulted. I asked Him why I felt so alone, so broken, so irreparable. I ended my prayer with an ultimatum. I told God that if He didn't give me the answers or give me a Word *that* night, I was going to go home and take my life.

Now, I don't recommend doing this at all, but God did speak to me that night. A girl who may have been in her mid-twenties walked up to me and began to speak. Do you know that she answered EVERY single question that I had asked God? She spoke to everything that I was saying to God. A girl that I had never ever met in my life, told me everything that I needed to hear from God.

To this day, I am so grateful for her obedience and willingness to speak what God was telling her to speak because it truly changed my life. In that moment, I felt again. I began to cry profusely because what she was saying was everything that I needed and more.

The Bible says that God will do exceeding abundantly above all that we can ask or think (Ephesians 3:10), and He did just that. And THAT was the moment that I decided maybe I should actually do what He says. Maybe I should start listening. And so, I did. I wish I had written down that date, but sadly, all I remember is that it was 2014. It was the moment that I decided to get up.

Friends, I think it may be time for you to get up too. If healing is what you desire, then you must be willing to get up. And if there is anything that I've learned about God, it's that He is polite. He isn't one of those people who forces you to do things that you don't want to; He makes it clear that there are repercussions for not doing things His way, but He never forces us to do anything.

He desires for you to be proactive in your pain. To get up. So, let's talk about what that looks like.

How to Be Proactive in Pain

I am not the only one in history that God has prompted to get up. In fact, I believe that God gave this same command to the Israelites back in the day. Jeremiah 29 demonstrates this perfectly.

The Israelites were in a season of captivity — a season they brought upon themselves as a result of their disobedience to God. What I found interesting was what God told them while they were in their captivity. In Jeremiah 29 God encourages them to be active in their circumstances. In my words, he told them to get up.

The text states,

> "this is what the Lord Almighty, the God of Israel, says to those I carried into exile from Jerusalem to Babylon: "Build houses and settle down; plant gardens and eat what they produce. Marry and have sons and daughters; find wives for your sons and give your daughters in marriage so that they too may have sons and daughters. Increase in number there; do not decrease. Also, seek the peace and prosperity of the city to which I have carried you into exile. Pray to the Lord for it, because if it prospers, you too will prosper" (vs. 4-7).

These people were in a season of darkness. They were in a season that they couldn't understand, didn't want to be in, and yet God told them to be fruitful and "build houses." That means to settle there. People don't just lay down roots somewhere to pick up two or three weeks later. God was telling them to continue to live their life even in their less than ideal situation.

This is the same prompt God was giving me. We all face circumstances that we don't like and that are sometimes out of our control, but what is within our control is our response. The way I see it, we have two options: to just sit there and feel miserable and sorry for ourselves or to get up and do something about it?

The Israelites could have moaned and groaned and hated being in captivity so much so that they did nothing. Or they could have maximized their circumstances and embraced where they were. Afterall, they were going to be there for seventy years instead of ten.

Now, I am not suggesting that you will be stuck or struggling for seventy years, but I am also not suggesting quick and immediate relief. I have no idea how long this test or trial will last for you. I do not know how long you will wrestle with pain or grief or loss. But if we continue reading Jeremiah 29:11, God makes a promise that should provide us immense comfort in whatever circumstance we find ourselves in.

He says, "For I know the plans I have for you," declares the Lord, "plans to prosper you and not to harm you, plans to give you hope and a future."

You see, sitting around and wallowing or eating or drinking or running to a guy or girl or partying or whatever else we often do to mask pain, avoid suffering, or run from darkness, is good for no one. God doesn't just magically snap His fingers and make pain disappear; though that would be easier, that is not how He is. That is not how He works. The situations we go through are meant to make us more like Christ. They are meant to transform us into His image, so if we never go through anything or if we never suffer like He did, how could we be transformed into His image?

My prayer is that God would enlighten you to the purpose for your pain, and that He would reveal to you the beauty that is going to be unmasked if you hold on a little longer. That He would capture your heart and compel you to get up and to move you towards action in your pain.

Chapter 5

Asking the Hard Questions

Can I be honest with you? I have no idea what I am doing. I have no idea how to write a book or what I am doing. If you're still reading at this point, well, all I can say is thank you. God is faithful, friends, and I pray that you would come into awareness of that truth in your life if you haven't already.

As I mentioned in the chapter "Sitting in Darkness," I said that this was going to be an internal exploration with God. That's what this section of the book is about. Now, we are getting into the thick of it. You thought finding the pain or your "it" was hard? Well, I'm so sorry, that was just the beginning.

Did you ever go to the beach when you were younger and take all of your tools and equipment? Or have you gone to the beach recently maybe with kids of your own and take toys? Maybe you didn't do either. Well, I'm sure you've been in Dollar Tree before. During the summer, Dollar Tree usually loads up with beach toys. They would have these bags with buckets to make sandcastles, yellow or blue shovels, and other toys that were perfect for playing in sand. The little shovels would be great for digging sand and placing it into your bucket. Well, we won't be dealing with little shovels here. As I thought about internal exploration, it's more like having a huge snow shovel, or better yet, a snow plowing machine. That's what it's like to explore with God. You get all the way into it. You aren't digging these cutesy baby holes. This is the real thing. I just thought it would be nice to warn you.

This internal exploration starts with asking the hard questions.

You've already acknowledged that there is pain or something that is not right within, but that is not enough. It is simply not enough to state how we are feeling or name it. Our goal here is to live a life that is spiritually, mentally, and emotionally healthy, so we must heed the advice in Hebrews 12 to "throw off anything that hinders us." That starts by asking the hard questions. It starts by asking why and what.

Why and What? What and Why?

I have a lot of wise people in my life that tell me a lot of things that I don't always want to hear. Sometimes they share advice that I never asked for, but I discovered I really needed it.

One day as I was sitting in my hotel room, I became extremely emotional out of the blue. I was traveling for work and burst into tears uncontrollably the moment I got settled in my room. Not even five minutes later, I received a text from someone that I really admire. It was the director of a Christian sports camp that I was a counselor at one summer. He texted me to check in with me. I knew better than to lie to him, so I was honest. I responded to his text, "I'm not okay but I'll be fine." I thought that maybe if I threw that last part in there, he would just leave it at that. Well, my phone started ringing. I thought, *really?! Now God?*

We were on the phone talking, and I just cried for most of the conversation. His tone was so endearing, but he challenged me.

He charged me to start reflecting. He told me to figure out the "why" and the "what." It was practical and helped me so much. He told me the "why" would help me figure out the reason I started crying. For example, maybe I started crying because I was sad. Then the "what" would help me figure out what happened the moment I began to feel sad. For example, maybe I had thought about the fact that I was in my hotel alone and I didn't want to be alone. So practical, but so necessary. The why and the what.

Now, you may be thinking well, I already figured out the "what" by naming it and addressing the pain. Or maybe you are still trying to figure out where I am going with this? I am wondering the same things, friends. I almost deleted this chapter too. But what God shared with me back then was that this kind of reflecting is necessary every day of my life.

Sure, I may have discovered the thing that was crippling me *(the darkness)* but the darkness affected me in different ways. There are things tied to the darkness that would manifest in different situations and moments in my life.

Let me break this down in a way that will hopefully make more sense. One day you wake up and you feel so amazing. You feel on top of the world like nothing can stop you, but then *bam,* out of nowhere that feeling turns into this deep anxiety. Maybe you received a text from a friend the moment prior. Maybe you received some news from work just a few moments prior. Maybe the barista's expression at the coffee shop rubbed you the wrong way.

There was a trigger to that switch in your demeanor. That is what "asking the hard questions" is all about. We must examine the situation and emotion from all possible angles.

I want to say that strong emotions are not bad at all. But if you recognize that the emotion is affecting your interactions and functioning, then it may be necessary to ask yourself questions to explore the emotion. The writer of Psalm 139 says, "Search me, God, and know my heart; test me and know my anxious thoughts. See if there is any offensive way in me, and lead me in the way everlasting."

We are searching our heart, and I would encourage you to repeat this to yourself. However you talk to God, ask him to help you as you search your heart.

As you do so, here are a list of questions that may aid you in this conquest:
- What am I feeling?
- Why am I feeling this way?
- What happened moments before I felt this way?
- Did a person or thing trigger me?
- Have I felt this before?
- When have I felt this before?

These questions are just a few that I might ask myself in moments that I am feeling strong emotions. I may start with "why" and "what" questions then begin to expand. These are not the only questions you can ask yourself, but the point is that you are basically interviewing yourself. You are not interrogating yourself. There is a difference. Interrogations are a bit intense and demanding, whereas the interview is a little slower and gentler. You are simply asking yourself a few questions to get to know yourself and what you are feeling a little better. I believe that as you ask God and begin to search, He will provide the answers that will help you move forward. He will help you live an examined life. Because as Socrates once said, "the unexamined life is not worth living."

The Examined Life

A visit to the dentist's office made me realize just how important it is to ask myself these hard questions. Let me preface by saying that the dentist is not my favorite place to go, so I try to avoid it if possible. Well, years had passed since my last cleaning, so my parents encouraged me to find a dentist in my area. *I'm good*, I thought. *I've been brushing regularly and flossing on occasion. I don't really need it.* However, I listened.

The next day I began my search. I found an office just ten minutes from my house and requested an appointment. They got back to me that same day and said that I could come in the next week. Fast forward to the day of my appointment, it was a great morning. I woke up, read my Bible, got dressed, and made my way to my 7:40 am appointment. After I found the office, I walked up, checked in, began to fill out some paperwork, and then was greeted to begin with some x-rays.

Everything was going well so far. I will admit that I was a bit hesitant because it was a new environment. But I had a great conversation with the hygienist. It was almost as if I had already known her. She then directed me to her station. She let me know that she was going to take more x-rays of my individual teeth and said that it would be a bit uncomfortable. *Cool, no worries.*

Once she finished the x-rays, she delivered me some news. She started by delivering the good news, "Wow, you have really beautiful teeth." But then came the bad, "However, I'm going to point out a few concerns that the dentist might address when she comes." "Uh okay," I said hesitantly. She pointed out what appeared to be cavities. She didn't point out just one or two spots; she pointed out a few! I won't state the number because I don't want you to judge me, but I was hurt. She told me not to worry, but it was too late for that. I couldn't believe that I had so many cavities. I had been doing everything right! I was brushing my teeth multiple times a day so I figured the report would be spotless.

She left the room to go get the dentist and she came back to point out on the x-rays what spots were the cavities. She let me know that they wouldn't have been noticeable because they were in between my teeth. I honestly didn't even know that it was possible to get cavities between your teeth. She went on to say that I was doing everything right but I wasn't flossing. She told me that just brushing didn't cut it.

It was at that moment that I began to hear the words of my childhood dentist ring in my head, "You need to start flossing Brittany." It's funny because every time I went to the dentist that is exactly what she would tell me. So, I would begin to floss just three days before my appointment so it would appear that I was flossing regularly. Eventually she stopped telling me to floss. I remember thinking that I had her fooled back then. But the truth is, I was the one who was fooled. I didn't realize the importance of something simple as flossing. I didn't realize that it would prevent "bad news" such as the news I received nearly 6 years later from my new dentist.

Oh how I wished I had listened. I just sank into the chair after the news. I was in disbelief that I had that many cavities. I was ashamed that I let it get that bad. *I should have searched for a dentist sooner*, I thought. But the stark reality was that it was too late. I couldn't turn back time and fix it; I had to live with my actions. I had to live with how bad things had gotten and choose to make a change moving forward.

This is the same truth I learned about asking the hard questions. Many times in life, we may get to a place and we are so confused because we can't seem to figure out when or how things got so bad. I didn't realize how many cavities could form because I wasn't aware of how flossing was a tool that could be used to help prevent them. In the same fashion, I didn't realize how bad things could get emotionally because I wasn't aware of how to actually work through what I was feeling. I wasn't aware of how to ask those questions.

I didn't realize that this kind of self-awareness and reflection was such a critical thing to engage in.

Google® defines *self-awareness* as the conscious knowledge of one's own character, feelings, motives, and desires. It is the capacity for introspection and the ability to recognize oneself as an individual separate from the environment and other individuals. So, let me ask you, on a scale from 0 to 10 with 10 being very self-aware and 0 being unaware, where would you rate yourself?

If you asked me years ago, I probably would have said a shaky 1, however, today, I'd say that I'm at maybe a solid 8 or 9. But it wasn't overnight that I got here; it took some patience and getting to know myself. I had to be intentional about learning myself and the things that trigger me. I also had to be honest about how I was feeling. And not only that, I had to block out the thoughts and opinions of society.

I believe society discourages this type of emotional awareness or honesty. Some people consider it "too feely" or "too much." Others think of it as something that shouldn't be discussed. In my generation that's what I've heard.

I think we've been subconsciously trained to ignore what we are truly feeling. Think about it, when someone asks, "How are you doing today?" what is your response? Many of us respond by saying "fine," or "good," regardless if it's true. You may be thinking that it's not that deep. But it really is. The more you speak over yourself that you are "fine," the more it becomes a natural response. The more you say, "I'm good," the more you train yourself to believe that you are really good.

I am not suggesting that you go tell any and everyone how you are feeling, I am simply encouraging you to pay attention to how you truly feel and to be honest about it. For example, if a grocery store clerk asks you "How are you today?" but you know it's been an awful day, saying "It hasn't been the best day but thanks for asking. How is your day going?", could be a simple but honest response. It seems simple, or maybe pointless, but this small switch in my language tremendously helped me to become more aware of my thoughts and feelings.

Maybe you are not sold on self-awareness and its importance yet. Let's take a look at the Bible. The Bible tells us in 1 Timothy 4:16 to keep a watch on ourselves because it will save both ourselves and others.

Did you think that this journey was going to be about you only? I know I sure did, but this journey is about others just as much as it is about you. Developing a deep self-awareness will help you to understand yourself and your emotions so much better, but it will also transform your relationships and how you interact with others and how you deal with problems and pain. I would say that is a pretty good deal.

Like many other steps in my journey, this was not an easy one either. I cried, and I gave up many, many times because it was just too difficult to navigate. However, once I truly made the decision to work through it, I slowly invited God into each and every area to examine those things with me.

2017

Time for a flashback.

After my assault, God led me on this journey of asking the hard questions. And what I found was anger, bitterness, confusion, hatred, and hopelessness to name a few. All things that are not like Him. I was angry with people. I was angry with myself. I was angry with God. I began to doubt my value and believed

I was no longer worthy to be married someday. I was bitter towards female friends in my life. I had a hard time trusting people. I felt shame. I felt rejected. I was insecure. I grew to be hypercritical of everything I did. I felt like a failure. I felt I had made such a big mistake by letting that happen to me.

All along, I was doing and trying to live right, yet all of those things were still festering and creating deeper, thicker roots. It wasn't until 2017, three years later, that I learned all of that was there. It was hard to learn all of that was in my heart. But once I did, I was able to move forward and learn how to clean it out. And that is exactly what you must do as well.

Think of it like cleaning out your attic or getting rid of all those college textbooks or maybe purging old clothes. It'll kind of be like that. And, no, it won't happen overnight. In fact, this process is something that I have to do every single day, but it is very important for us in our pursuit of freedom. As Christians, we are called to be imitators of Christ; therefore, our job is to try to make sure our heart, our thoughts, and our actions align with His. I'm not suggesting that we become perfect, because that's simply not something we are capable of being. However, I am suggesting that there are things that are not like Him that hide within us that we must rid ourselves of if we are to reflect his image.

The New Testament reveals many of these things. Ephesians 4:31 says to get rid of "all bitterness, rage and anger, brawling and slander, along with every form of malice." In 1 Peter 2:1 it says, "therefore, rid yourselves of all malice and all deceit, hypocrisy, envy, and slander of every kind." Unforgiveness is also one that the Bible reminds us to let go of. The Bible says that we should forgive as Christ forgave (Colossians 3:13). I would like to also suggest that getting rid of pride, shame, or guilt will be critical. The list could go on, however, I just wanted to point out a few.

Maybe you are reading this and you realize that you have been having a reaction to something and can't put a finger on it. Just as I invited God into those places, you must be willing to do the same. He is the Ultimate Healer. He can change any thought or emotion. Even if you consider yourself one of the most stubborn people in the world, He can reach you and soften your heart too.

By no means is this process fun, however, as I mentioned before you must remember that this is for your growth and transformation. It is hard work you may not want to do or get tired of doing. But it has tremendous benefits for your relationship with God, your relationship with others, and your health.

Now, I call you to action. I don't know what things or emotions you recognize that are disrupting your life or maybe hurting your relationships, but I do encourage you to ask God to search your heart (Psalm 139: 23). Ask Him to guide you to discover what may be in your heart. If you recognize that there are things that don't belong there, then you should begin digging. Hop on that snowplow with God and get to work.

You'll probably hear this multiple times in every chapter: this is not easy work. However, I would suggest that it is worth it and necessary to make any progress in this journey. I am rooting for you still. You got this!

Now would be a great time to pause with your reading. I encourage you to just close the pages for a moment and go spend quiet time with the Lord. I believe that there is healing that is going to happen in your life once you invite Him in. Ask Him to reveal the things that are hiding in your heart. Ask Him to show you the things that are not like Him. Ask Him to search your heart. You may also ask yourself, what things am I still holding on to? Are my interactions with others healthy or is there a wound there? Do I have any stubbornness toward someone in my life?

You may not recognize what is in your heart right away, but I do trust that the same God who helped me identify these things will lead and guide you as well.

I'd like to offer another suggestion here and that is to purchase a journal or start an online personal journal for yourself. A journal will allow you to write or type out your thoughts, feelings, and emotions. It will allow you to keep a log of the things that you find and express how you are feeling about it. I used my journal to write out prayers and thoughts to God about where I currently was in my life. I used it to let Him know how I felt about my assault. I used it to let Him know when I wanted to give up. I used it to clarify and declutter my mind. I used it to grow closer to the Lord and to remember each and every step that I took forward.

It became something that traveled with me everywhere I went. If I needed to stop and write, I would whip out my journal and pour out my heart on the pages that no one but myself and God would see. It was the place I could detail my juiciest secrets, deepest regrets, and most painful days. It was my reminder to keep going. It was a reminder to surrender this journey to the Lord. And that is just what I found that I had to do next: surrender.

Chapter 6

Surrendering

When you hear the word *surrender*, what is the first thought that comes to your mind? For me, I immediately think about someone with their hands up, giving up a fight. I asked a friend and she broke out in song with her hands lifted singing, "I surrender, I surrender, I want to know you more." This is a popular worship song by *Hillsong* called "I Surrender." This is the exact surrender I want you to think of. Hands up or hands open, ready to surrender everything to God. I told you in the last chapter this was going to be internal exploration with God, right? Well, here goes nothing.

Wikipedia defines *surrender* in regard to religion, as completely giving up your own will and subjecting your thoughts, ideas, and actions to the will and teachings of God or submission.

As a believer in Christ we are called to submit ourselves to God, but if I'm being honest, that's not the easiest thing to do. It's one of those things that is "easier said than done." Well, at least for me, it is anyway.

If we flashback to those college days that I mentioned before, I remember a moment that I thought that I was surrendering, but honestly, I was just seeking a quick fix to the funky mood I was in. I made a declaration to God like "God, Daddy, I am done. I am tired. Please take this pain away. I won't do x, y, or z again." Then once the pain I felt was gone, I turned right back around and called this guy or went to that party or was ready to turn up with my friends. I was using God. I didn't really want a relationship with Him; I just wanted what He could give me. I wanted to feel good, to be happy, and to do whatever I wanted to do.

This thinking was so detrimental, and I didn't even realize it. It wasn't until one night sitting in my apartment locked up in my room with a snotty nose and red eyes journaling, that I realized that I had to change the way I was living.

"Lord I am lost, broken, confused, and just in pain. I'd rather be anywhere except here on earth. I don't know who I am, why I am, or what I am. I am hurting ... I feel so alone yet so surrounded. Please, Lord, help me to stop these feelings, stop this pain. Why do I hurt so much, why do I feel this way? Please, just please help me. I will do anything if you just make this pain go away. I am trapped, entangled within this broken girl, and I can't get away from her. I can't let go. She is not me. I don't know who she is, but she has taken over my body and mind. Help me, please help me to get away from here, from her. I don't want to be here anymore, and it terrifies me. I don't want to be here, and the pain is just growing unbearable ... I don't know who I've become, please help. PLEASE!"

These are the exact words that I scribbled in my journal on February 8, 2015. This was my declaration of surrender. I was lost, I was broken, and I was depressed. I was struggling to find my way back to who I knew myself to be. Or at least who I thought I was. It was time to lay those things, those dead seeds, that pain, those events down and surrender them to the Lord.

It was time to release. It was time to let go.

Let Go

One of the best demonstrations of letting go, other than Jesus, that I have read about is that of Abraham in the Bible. His personal story is found in Genesis.

Abraham, who had been waiting for his wife to conceive a child, after a Word from the Lord, finally saw that Word come to life. At the age of 90, Sarah bore Abraham a son and he was named Isaac (Genesis 21:2-3). Now, can you imagine waiting until you are that old to have a child? That's a bit long to wait, and I haven't birthed a baby yet, but I can only imagine how much worse that is to do at the age of 90. However, God made it happen.

As we continue reading the text, we see Isaac growing up and then the Lord calls out to Abraham and asks him to take his son Isaac and go to the region of Moriah. He wanted him to sacrifice him there as a burnt offering (Genesis 22).

One thing I didn't realize until after reading this passage is that God told Moses to sacrifice him as a burnt offering. As one of the guest pastors at my church pointed out one Sunday, "That meant Abraham wasn't going to get his son back." A burnt offering meant that you would not receive anything in return, all of the offering was to be completely burned (Leviticus 1:9).

I can't even begin to imagine the thoughts that Abraham may have had. He had to wait until he was 100 years old and his wife 90 to have a son, and then was asked to sacrifice him. The one thing that he waited and waited for, he was being asked to give to the Lord. Nonetheless, Abraham obeyed. Abraham walked up the mountain with everything that he needed for the sacrifice and prepared to offer his son.

As I thought about this moment in Abraham's life, the song "I Lean Not on My Own Understanding" by Leon Timbo came to mind. The song talks about climbing a mountain with hands that are wide open, releasing everything to God. This is exactly the heart posture that I believe Abraham had as he climbed that mountain. He was being asked to do something that I imagine was not easy at all. However, he made the choice to let go. He made the choice not to take control of his son's life. He made the choice to obey. And as he made the choice to surrender and let go, the Lord provided a ram for the sacrifice (Genesis 22:13). His son was saved because of his choice to surrender.

Each and every day that we wake up, we have the choice of what we are going to hold onto. Every day, not some days. Not only the days when we are feeling great. Not only the days when we are happy. But every day we have the opportunity to choose what we are going to walk around with. For me, there were many things that I was holding onto in my journey that I honestly had no business holding onto. I was carrying around bitterness, anger, low self-esteem, jealousy, resentment, sadness, and so many more emotions in my hands. And I held a mean grip on it. I wouldn't let it go just yet. And because of this, I was hindering myself from moving anywhere close to freedom.

It took me awhile to grasp the totality of this because quite frankly, when everything is dark and seems hopeless, it doesn't quite feel like you have control over anything at all. But that is the beauty and encouragement that I get to share with you today. You do have control over how and what you hold onto. You have the ability to let go and surrender just as Abraham did.

You have to make that conscious choice each and every day to let go of those things you are holding onto. I had to make the choice to surrender everything to God if I wanted to make any progress towards freedom. I have to make this same choice today. And every time that I do this, it makes the next time just a little bit easier. This is because it's a training process. What you rehearse and repeat becomes a habit.

It's often said that if you do something for twenty-one days you create a habit. I am not exactly sure how legitimate that claim is as far as the number of days, however, I do believe that if you continue to do something long enough, it eventually becomes a habit. The most common example I can think of is brushing your teeth. The more you do it, it becomes natural to do it every day. The more you choose to surrender to God each day, the more natural it will become. That is what I am finding to be true. It becomes a mindset and a way of doing things. If I constantly wake up and remind myself or speak over myself that I am going to surrender [*insert thing*], I am training my mind to let go of those things. The same goes for you.

And it is not a grudging surrender either. People can tell you what you need to do. I can share with you what worked for me. However, it will all be meaningless unless your surrender is out of desperation. You have to want in your heart to be well. I have found that the more I desire to be well, the greater the cry of desperation, and in turn the easier it is to surrender. I had to get to a point that I desperately wanted to be well and I believed that I could be well. Once I got to that point, surrender became slightly easier. I believe that king David found this to be true as well.

In a time when David was hiding in the wilderness from his son Absalom, he cries out, "O God, you are my God; earnestly I seek you; my soul thirsts for you; my flesh faints for you, as in a dry and weary land where there is no water" (Psalm 63:1).

David was king of the united kingdom of Israel at the time of writing this Psalm. He was the king. He had everything. He could've easily ran to one of his wives or his money. This time he didn't because he knew it all was meaningless. Instead, he sought God. David had gotten to a point of desperation realizing that nothing else could help or satisfy him. He knew that God was the ONLY one that could satisfy his soul.

David did not live a perfect life of surrendering to God first and foremost. Surrendering was a behavior that he learned after many mistakes and failures in his life. Similarly, **I didn't choose God first, but eventually I grew to that place where my desperation was so strong that it drove me to surrender.** Regardless of what that would look like, I had to surrender.

The Ultimate Example

So, we've looked at Abraham, David, and me, now let us look to the ultimate example of surrender found in Matthew 26:36-39.

> "Then Jesus went with them to a place called Gethsemane, and he said to his disciples, "Sit here, while I go over there and pray." And taking with him Peter and the two sons of Zebedee, he began to be sorrowful and troubled. Then he said to them, 'My soul is very sorrowful, even to death; remain here, and watch with me.' And going a little farther he fell on his face and prayed, saying, 'My Father, if it be possible, let this cup pass from me; nevertheless, not as I will, but as you will.'"

Even Jesus didn't really want to surrender. He asks God, "if it's possible let this cup pass from me." He is asking God if at all possible, could He save humanity another way. Jesus knew the suffering He was about to endure on the cross and that he had to choose to surrender his life. Nevertheless, He still says, "not as I will, but as you will."

This is a perfect example and challenge to surrender. Jesus was fully God and fully human. Being fully human means that He can empathize with our fear to surrender. No, He didn't want to surrender; He didn't want to give up his life, but He knew that He had to. He knew that there was no other way for me and you to be saved but by the shedding of His blood. That is simply amazing.

If you are tired of being stuck, tired of being angry, sad, depressed, or even bitter, it may be time for you to surrender. You've made it this far in the book, so I believe you want to be well. I believe that you, too, are wanting to walk in freedom.

Now, my surrender, Abraham's surrender, David's surrender, and Jesus' surrender all looked very different. Yours will look different as well, however, you know better than anyone what you need to surrender to God in order to start walking towards freedom. You already named it. So, it's time to surrender it.

I pray that even now as you read this, God will bring to your mind or lay on your heart what He needs you to surrender. I pray that those things He brought to your mind in the previous chapter resurface. I pray your eyes would be opened to all that is holding you back from true freedom.

And I understand, it can be very nerve wracking to surrender because you may not know what it looks like, but remember that surrender is not meant to hurt you, and neither is your pain. The Bible tells us, "For I know the plans I have for you," declares the Lord, "plans to prosper you and not to harm you, plans to give you hope and a future." (Jeremiah 29:11)

Surrender is about releasing your journey to the Lord. It is about walking to the Lord with all that baggage and letting Him take control of it. It is about His will being done.

Last Thoughts

To finish off this chapter, I just want you to know that your pain is not something that will be unbearable forever. I truly believed that it would always be bad and that I would always be stuck. However, it is not how things will always be or something that you have to grow accustomed to. Yes, you will still experience pain in your life, but with every painful experience or hurt you encounter it is a new opportunity to surrender again and again and again. And as you do so, you will experience the freedom that you are desperately wanting. You will have peace amid your pain, freedom amid your pain, and hope amid your pain. And believe me, it is right within your grasp, but you must go ahead and surrender it all to God.

So now, I ask, are you willing to surrender to God? Regardless of what that looks like, are you willing?

If so, let Him know. With your hands raised up, give up the fight so that He can take over. It's time my friends. It no longer serves a purpose in your life. Your bitterness has to go. Your anger has to go. Your anxiety has to go. Your fear has to go. God wants it.

And once you hand it over, you may feel vulnerable and exposed, but that is the best place to be, because that is where God can work. God is a gentleman. He waits patiently for us to invite Him in rather than inviting Himself in. So, I ask again. Whatever your "it" is, whatever thing you named, will you surrender it?

If books could have a long pause or take a commercial break, I would insert it here. But again, I encourage you to take some time to figure out whether or not you feel that you are ready to surrender, and it is okay if you do not feel that you are ready at this moment. God will continue to wait, because as I said before, He is a gentleman.

I did not surrender immediately. In fact, God had to work on my heart for quite some time before I actually surrendered. So, take your time, but remember the ball is in your court. If you want freedom, if you want restoration of your hope, joy, and peace, you absolutely must surrender. And if it eases your mind, you can think of it like getting on an airplane, if you have been on one. You have planned a trip and may have concerns or fears, nevertheless, you board your flight and get comfortable in your seat. You surrender to that plane and to those pilots and you trust them to get you to your destination safely.

Maybe you've never been on a plane. Well, think about a teacher. You don't question your professor or teacher. You don't check their credentials and where they got their degree(s). You trust that what they are teaching you is accurate and true and will help you reach the next level you need to reach. You surrender and allow them to lead you in learning.

These are practical examples, but nonetheless, real examples of surrender in different contexts. If you can surrender and trust these people that you do not know to get you to places safely or to teach you correctly, I believe that you, too, can trust and surrender to the Creator of the Universe who you do know. So, one last time: Will you surrender to God?

I'm hoping you said "yes" but if not, that's okay too. I believe that as you continue to read you will be compelled to surrender because once you are able to grasp all that is waiting for you on the other side of surrender you might just drop everything and flee to God. I prayed it over you, so I'm believing it will happen. I cannot wait. Because after you surrender, I really think you are going to enjoy this next chapter. It's a fun one, I promise.

Chapter 7

Fighting

Assuming that you've decided to get up and you've decided to surrender as well, it's time to keep working. It's time to get in the ring and fight. Now is the time where you get to push back against the enemy. Now is the time that you partner with God and defeat the enemy. Now is the time that we take back what the enemy stole. I am just so excited for this. If you've made it this far in reading this book, I hope you are excited too. Satan has tried it for too long. He has been in control for too long. But it's time to take that control back.

    My good friend/mentor/sister inspired this chapter because it wasn't until her word of encouragement that I realized that fighting is what I was doing in my journey. It's what I do every day in my life. It is the same thing that you must do as well. And it's okay if you aren't the best or strongest fighter in the world, because you'll still win either way.

How is that you might ask?

Well there are two reasons. One reason is that in boxing, strength isn't necessarily a deciding factor. After some research, I found that skill/technique and stamina are much more important in boxing than strength. The second reason is that God's got you covered with the strength portion anyway. But we will get to that part later. I needed to add this little tidbit because I realize how often I've associated fighting with strength. But here in this book and this chapter specifically, I want strength to be the last worry you have.

Talking about fighting makes me think of moments with my older brother growing up. We were always fighting, and I always lost. I was a feisty little girl who wouldn't give up the fight. In fact, if I am honest, I always picked the fight. I was an annoying little sister. I would annoy my brother by pointing my finger just inches from his face and say, "I'm not touching you." Or I would punch him in the arm and say "punch buggy no punch back" even when I really didn't see a Volkswagen Beetle at all. That used to be such a fun game. But in a sense, I actually set myself up to get into a fight with my brother.

Looking back, it was pretty hilarious, but if someone was doing that to me, I probably would've wanted to fight them too. Well, maybe not because I'm not a fighter. I loathe confrontation. But if someone was taunting me and annoying me constantly, I would want it to stop without a doubt. And, so, this is the same way I had to get with both myself and the enemy.

You might be confused by me saying that I had to get that way with myself but one thing that you will learn is that sometimes you have to wage war against yourself too.

The Fight AGAINST Yourself

Would you agree that in times of trouble you've found yourself trying to run to the thing that is most familiar? The thing that provides you the most comfort. C'mon, be honest. You know that thing. Maybe it's a person, a food, a habit? It's the first thing that comes to mind when things start to get crazy. Maybe that's God for you, but I'm going to be honest and just say that He's not always the first thing I run to.

I've shared many of the things I've run to and sometimes still run to, the Dairy Queen® Reese's® Peanut Butter Cup® Blizzard®, the steak, the Oreos®, purple Doritos®? I could go on, but nine times out of ten, I will run to food first. It's not the best coping habit. But one thing that I have learned about us humans is that we tend to run to what is most familiar, especially in times of chaos and confusion.

This chapter serves as another warning to you. You will be tempted to run to what's comfortable when things get hard. When you get tired and overwhelmed, you may get tempted to shut down. But this is a fight. This is a fight against ourselves. A fight against our flesh. I know what you want to do. I know that you want to turn back, and it's okay if you do because of grace. However, you will not get anywhere by allowing yourself to revert to the same bad habits that didn't do any good for you in the first place. Hear me out.

Back in college I struggled so hard with this. And I failed many, many times. I backslid several times.

I tried to tell myself "no." But it didn't always work out that way. My passion and desperation to be better weren't greater than the desires of my flesh. I thought I couldn't handle it, so I went for the quick remedy instead.

Even though I knew that my healing couldn't be found in those things, even though I knew what was not good for me, and even though I knew it was just a temporary solution, I still went back to the same things. Romans 8:5-7 says,

> "Those who live according to the flesh have their minds set on what the flesh desires; but those who live in accordance with the Spirit have their minds set on what the Spirit desires. The mind governed by the flesh is death, but the mind governed by the Spirit is life and peace. The mind governed by the flesh is hostile to God; it does not submit to God's law, nor can it do so."

I clearly had my mind on what the flesh desired, and I had to fight my flesh. I had to learn how to reject its desires. Now, not all desires are bad. However, in the wrong context they can be considered bad. Let's use sex as an example.

I am currently not married. I am single as a pringle as some would say. Being that I am not married, if I found myself in a rut and called a male friend over to help with this, then I am acting out the desires of my flesh. You see, God has nothing against sex when it comes to married folks. But I just said that I am single, right? So, if I were to do this, I am acting out in what my flesh desires. Got it?

Similarly, ice cream is not inherently bad, but if I am using it as a coping mechanism to avoid facing what I don't want to face, then I am acting out on my flesh's desires. I am sure you get it by now.

You know better than anyone else what you run to as a coping mechanism or to escape, so the challenge here is simple: say no.

You will want comfort. You may tell yourself that just one more drink won't hurt. You will want to give up. You might want to stay complacent and shut down when life gets tough. The possibilities are endless, but if whatever you find yourself running to does not contribute to your growth and help you get better spiritually, mentally, or physically, walk away. Say no.

The Bible tells us that God's power is perfected in weakness (2 Corinthians 12:9). It tells us that when we are weak, He is strong (2 Corinthians 12:10). Therefore, when you feel weak and ready to give in, hold on to that scripture. Declare it over yourself. Look that thing in the eye and say *no! You will not win!*

This may sound silly, but it worked for me. There were so many times that I bought something that I knew I didn't need. There were times that I went to stuff my face and had to spit the food out because I wasn't really hungry. It's a real struggle.

Let me end with this story because to this very day it is funny to me, but I want to show you how God shut me down quickly one day in college. I didn't even have to tell myself "no." He did it for me.

2015

There was a night some of my friends were going to this bar and grill for college night towards the end of my sophomore year. I knew I didn't need to go, but I told myself that it would be okay. Just one night out wouldn't hurt.

I hopped in the car and tagged along. This was a time where I was making progress in my journey. I had made my declaration of surrender early that year. I was actively trying to live better and get rid of all the toxic emotions and patterns I had developed. I was going to church more and growing in my relationship with the Lord; however, I went anyway.

We got to the bar and it was pretty nice. This was my first time there. They had pool tables, so I hung out in that area. I told myself that I wouldn't dance or drink. I would just hang out and try to enjoy myself. That lasted for two seconds. Eventually, I found someone I knew that was of age to buy me a drink. I finished the first drink and got another. Midway through my second drink, a girl I knew came over for what I thought was going to be just small talk. She was someone I knew through a mutual friend. She walked over but the conversation wasn't what I expected.

Girl: Hey Brittany!
Me: Hey, how are you?
Girl: I'm good, you gonna be at church on Sunday?

I don't even know if I mumbled a word back. I was so shocked. Here we are in a bar on a Thursday night, me with a drink in my hand, and she asks me about church!

I felt so convicted at that moment. It seems small, but it messed me up. I didn't even pick that drink back up. I just wanted to go home. I couldn't believe that she had just asked me that. I wasn't mad or upset, just lost for words. I didn't quite know what to think or say. I probably just said, "Yes I will," and then went about my way.

I was on my second drink and had she not come over, I probably would've gotten another and another and another, and before long I would've been right back to drowning my sorrows. She stopped me. I believe that God truly used her that night to teach me about myself. I was doing so well, and I just let myself fall into those old patterns again.

Looking back, I didn't do the best job of denying my flesh, but just like any hard-headed kid, I had to learn the hard way. I had to learn from my failures and mistakes. And that is exactly what I did. After that weekend, I tried my best to get back on the right path. I tried to get back to putting myself and my healing first. I failed many times, but eventually, I was able to focus. I was able to tell myself "no" by inviting the Holy Spirit in and being honest about my weakness. I had to be reminded of the reason that I started out my journey in the first place. It was because of my brokenness and the darkness that I desperately wanted to get rid of.

I was tempted for a moment thinking that I could still dabble in the old things and be fine, but I wasn't fine at all. I was still struggling, and I tempted my flesh by going to an environment that I already knew was a trigger for myself.

This is where it becomes critical to fight against your flesh. You, like me, may be tempted to go revert to those old ways. You may be tempted to go back to that thing, whatever it may be, thinking that it will be a source of comfort, but it is a lie that you must not let yourself believe. Or you may be tempted to try something new, but I urge you to be cautious and ask yourself why you are seeking out x, y, or z.

In my experience, I knew the things that I ran to for comfort and the things that were not "good" for me, but I made excuses like *it won't hurt if I do this just once more.* That's a lie too. Refuse, refuse, refuse to let yourself go there. With the help of the Holy Spirit, you can overcome your flesh. You can! And remember, "the mind governed by the flesh is death, but the mind governed by the Spirit is life and peace." If you want that freedom, you have to be willing to fight against your flesh.

There is also another fight that we are going to talk about. In fact, there are many fights that we will decipher, but the next one to address is the fight FOR yourself.

The Fight FOR Yourself

The fight for yourself is the fight for your freedom. It's the fight that says "I won't give up." You are fighting *for* yourself by fighting *against* yourself.

In 2019, I learned the true meaning of fighting *for* yourself. Several events in my life had triggered me to go on another spiral. The darkness was back, and it was stronger than it had ever been before. I thought that I had finally addressed the pain. I was doing the digging from the events of the past and I had surrendered, but yet again I found myself in this pit surrounded by darkness. Whenever I laid down to sleep, it felt like I had that bus sitting on top of my chest again. Whenever I woke up, I couldn't seem to get out of my bed. The suicidal thoughts came back. The darkness surrounded me, I didn't want to be here.

On March 2, 2019, I scribbled in my journal, "Tonight is one of those nights that I'd rather be dead. The weight I feel is too heavy. Are you still here? Are you still willing to take my burdens? I can't take it. I can't. I am trying to push through, but I feel like I can't. I can't breathe. I feel like me believing isn't enough anymore. I don't know what I am doing but I am trying. Please help me. Please."

Yet again, I was in this dark place wondering how in the world I was going to get out of it. But this time it was different.

This time, I made the choice to fight FOR myself. If you look back to what I wrote in my journal, I said, "I don't know what I am doing <u>BUT I am trying</u>." I wasn't going to give up. I was going to wake up every day and do something about it. You see, this is the distinction between the first time and the last. The first time, I just sat there and allowed myself to be defeated. I allowed the enemy to have control over my voice, my thoughts, and any inkling of control that I thought I had. This time, I put my foot down and I said, "Absolutely not!" I got ugly toward satan. I had to let him know that he couldn't have me. Not this time! Not ever again.

Just recently I watched a movie on Netflix® called "Same Kind of Different as Me." It was such a good movie and based on a true story. But there was one point in the movie where one of the men, Denver, said to his friend, "When you is precious to God, you become important to satan. Watch your back." I remember letting out a long, drawn out *wow* after hearing that.

It's so true! When you are important to God, you are important to satan as well. If you haven't caught on by now, he doesn't want to see you flourish. He doesn't want to see you free. He would much rather see you in bondage, sitting in that darkness feeling hopeless and defeated. This is why the fight *for* yourself is so important.

Let me ask you some real questions. Do you value yourself? Do you believe that you are worthy of freedom? Do you believe that God has plans for your life?

If you subconsciously answered no to any of these questions, I think it may be time to take a pause and ask God to allow you to see yourself how He sees you. Because it is going to be extremely hard to fight for yourself when you do not truly value yourself.

This is another distinction between the two periods of darkness that I encountered. When I was in college, I had little to no self-worth. I didn't value myself. However, as a young adult, I can now say that I do truly value myself. But it wasn't until after I asked God to help me see that true worth. And I had to remind myself daily of my worth through God's Word.

I had this huge whiteboard that I still own to this day where I had to write out affirmations. Each morning when I woke up, that board was directly across from my bed to remind me just how valuable I was. How valuable I am. If I didn't value myself, I wouldn't have been able to overcome this bout of darkness. Likewise, if you don't value yourself, it will be hard for you to overcome it. Or maybe you're like me and you know that you are valuable because the Bible says so, but it's not the easiest thing to believe sometimes.

One thing I have learned is that knowledge is not always enough. Sometimes we have all the right knowledge and information but until our mind is aligned with it, it is impossible to believe. I believe this may have been what the man in Mark 9:24 may have been alluding to. The text says, "the father of the child cried out and said with tears, "Lord, I believe; help my unbelief.""

This man's son had a spirit within him that was torturing his son to the point where it was hard for him to function. Prior to the man's statement, Jesus said to the man, "If you can believe, all things are possible to him who believes." (Mark 9:23)

I believe that this man was showing the discrepancy that many of us show today. We believe. We know that God can do anything. Maybe we've seen miracles or read about all of the miracles, signs, and wonders. However, when it comes to ourselves, it's a bit hard to believe that it can happen for us. We have some unbelief that is living right beside the belief that we have in Him.

And believe me, I am not just talking to you. I am talking to myself even now as I write these words. But let me tell you something. You are valuable whether you can see that now or not.

So, I encourage you to lay this book down for a few moments and spend time with God. Whatever that looks like for you, spend time communicating with Him, asking Him to show you what He sees when He looks at you and asking Him to allow you to see yourself as worth it.

Telling you that you have to fight for yourself is meaningless unless you believe you are worth it. And even if you consider yourself someone who already values yourself, I still encourage you to take this time, as we all have some kind of view about ourselves that may not necessarily align with God's view of us. We all have something that is or may be trying to work against us.

The Fight WITH God Against the Enemy

Sitting in a Starbucks® reading my Bible in a year devotional one day, I understood the fight *with* God much differently. It's a fight that He invites us to partner with Him. The God of the universe, the most high, the all-powerful God, wants you and me on His team. We are co-laborers with Him.

The book of Ephesians is a letter that is written by Paul to believers in Christ that demonstrates this. In Ephesians 6, Paul introduces this principle of a spiritual battle. He starts his letter, "finally, be strong in the Lord and in his mighty power." I think that Paul's selection of words here is so unique. He instructs them to be strong, but to be strong *in* the Lord. Not in yourself. Not in the world. We need to be strong in the Lord. We need to partner with God in order to fight our battles.

Paul continues the letter by stating that once we put on the full armor of God, once we partner with Him, we have the ability, through His mighty power, to take a stand against the devil's schemes. We have the opportunity to start fighting.

I like how the amplified version of the Bible puts it. It states, "put on the full armor of God, so that you may be able to *successfully* stand up against the schemes and the strategies and the deceits of the devil." (Ephesians 6:11)

How I interpret this is that we can only win the fight against the devil when we fight *with* God. Simply fighting in and of my own strength will leave me defeated. *Got it?* Let's continue to read Paul's instructions.

"Therefore, put on the complete armor of God, so that you will be able to [successfully] resist and stand your ground in the evil day [of danger], and having done everything [that the crisis demands], to stand firm [in your place, fully prepared, immovable, victorious]" (vs. 13).

Paul has told us not once but twice to put on the complete armor of God. What's Paul getting at? I believe he wants to stress to us how important it is to wear or have this full armor, not just occasionally but every day. He wants us to know that we cannot possibly go into a fight against darkness without the armor of God. Paul ends with this:

"Because of this, you must wear all the armor that God provides so you're protected as you confront the slanderer, for you are destined for all things and will rise victorious.

Put on truth as a belt to strengthen you to stand in triumph. Put on holiness as the protective armor that covers your heart. Stand on your feet alert, then you'll always be ready to share the blessings of peace.

In every battle, take faith as your wrap-around shield, for it is able to extinguish the blazing arrows coming at you from the Evil One! Embrace the power of salvation's full deliverance, like a helmet to protect your thoughts from lies. And take the mighty razor-sharp Spirit-sword of the spoken Word of God.

Pray passionately in the Spirit, as you constantly intercede with every form of prayer at all times. Pray the blessings of God upon all his believers." (Ephesians 6: 13 - 18, TPT)

These are our weapons to fight this fight *with* God and against Satan. And guess what? We win!

Keep Fighting

Fighting is going to be required in order to overcome the "it" that you've named... In order to overcome the darkness.

It is a fight that has to be fought *with* God and against the enemy. It is a fight that has to be fought against your flesh and its desires and tendencies to run to the easy or comforting things. It is a fight that has to be fought *for* yourself. Your life is a life worth living to the fullest. It is a life that God wants you to enjoy and prosper in.

I remember a friend approaching me one day after church and asking how I was doing. I assumed she already knew so I didn't intend to lie. I honestly told her, "I'm not okay, but I'm fighting." She encouraged me to keep fighting and I assured her that I would.

As someone speaking from experience, I assure you that freedom is on the other side of your fight, a testimony to share is on the other side of your fight, and victory comes from your fight. As tough as it may seem, as difficult as it is, as weak as you may feel, don't give up on yourself. You are worth living. You are important. You are needed.

So, if you are ready, let's get into some of the essential tools needed. Many of these tools will overlap what Paul has already shown us that we need, while others will supplement them. Nonetheless, they are all essential tools that we need for the lifting.

PART 3

The Lifting
Essential Tools Needed

He lifted me out of the slimy pit
out of the mud and mire;
Psalm 40:2 NIV

Chapter 8

A Transformed Mind

"Do not conform to the pattern of this world, but be transformed by the renewing of your mind. Then you will be able to test and approve what God's will is – his good, pleasing, and perfect will" (Romans 12:2, NIV).

When I graduated from college, I was handed a cross. It wasn't a paper cross or something lightweight. It was a metal cross with Romans 12:2 attached to it. Don't worry, this wasn't handed to me with the fake diploma they hand you when you walk across the stage, though that would've been nice. It was handed to me by the campus pastor of the college ministry I was a part of in college.

For a long time, I didn't get it. I didn't understand why I was handed that cross with that specific scripture, but to this day I know that it was no accident. I'm not sure if everyone was given that scripture or if it was specific to me, but I believe that God was speaking through my pastor and his wife.

This scripture has continued to be important at every single stage of my life. It was useful then and it is useful today. Always has been and it always will be. For me, a lot of my battles are in my mind. They are in my thoughts. If there's one thing in my life that the enemy attacks more than anything else, it's my thought life. Of course, he picks at other things, but my mind, that's probably another book. But don't worry, I'll be straightforward and get to the point.

Transforming your mind starts with the realization that you play a part in the thoughts and choices that you make. It is about aligning your thoughts with God's perfect will for you, it is about dwelling on things that are good for you, and it's about your peace. When we take control and take responsibility for our thoughts, it is then that we partner with God and the lifting begins.

The Wrong Thoughts

The devil attacks us in many different ways. One of those ways is in our thought life. In Joyce Meyer's devotional, *My time with God*, she talks about how one morning she knew that the devil was attacking her and one thing that she had to do was to replace the wrong thoughts with good ones. That is the key to transforming your mind. We want to get rid of the wrong thoughts—the ones that are not like God—and replace them with the right ones.

The thoughts that speak against our identity in Christ and the thoughts that speak against our purpose and our relationships are the wrong thoughts. And while I can't dissect your mind and tell you what thoughts you need to replace or get rid of, I have a simple solution for you. If it does not align with the Word of God, it needs to go.

If it says that you are less than, unworthy, unlovable, or unfixable, it needs to go. If it says that God is not with you, that He doesn't care, or that He doesn't love you, it needs to go. If it says that God has left you, He isn't listening, or no one cares about what you have to say, it needs to go. If it says you are alone, incapable, or don't need people, it needs to go.

We all have these thoughts. We all have self-deprecating thoughts. We all hear the lies of the enemy. We all are attacked in some way. Does it make it easier? Not at all. But each and every day you and I have a choice of what we are going to listen to. Will we believe the lies that we constantly hear? Or will we follow the example of Joyce Meyer and replace those wrong thoughts with truth?

One thought that I had in the initial stages of my journey was that I would never be free from the darkness. I had made it up in my mind that I was going to be stuck forever. I believed it. Months passed and nothing was changing. I was doing all the "right" things, however, I was still believing that I couldn't be healed or free. I was dead set on the fact that my life would be that way forever and I just had to deal with it. And because that was my belief, that's how my life remained. I remained hopeless because I couldn't bring myself to tear down that thought.

In 2 Corinthians 5:17 it states, "We demolish arguments and every pretension that sets itself up against the knowledge of God, and we take captive every thought to make it obedient to Christ."

This is what I believe Meyer was referring to. She was tearing down the thoughts that were against the knowledge of God and making them obedient to Christ.

Anytime we feel our mind wandering to that negative, fearful or hopeless place, we must also tear it down and instead combat it with the Word of God.

Now that we've gotten that straightened out. I want to talk about your peace. Because your peace needs protecting.

Protect Your Peace

For a long time, I kept feeling God tell me, "Protect your peace." No matter what I was doing, I felt His prompting, "Protect your peace." I really had no idea why He kept telling me that or what it meant until a moment my peace was rocked.

A lot of times, peace is the very first thing that is shaken and stirred when things in life are rough. When trouble comes, peace can go right out the door.

There was a point in my life where so much was going on and I didn't know how to handle it. The pressure that I was feeling was too great for me to bear. My mind was all over the place. I felt like I couldn't think straight. I was extremely anxious. I felt that I couldn't quiet the enemy. He had my peace in his grasp and wouldn't loosen the grip. I struggled to take back the peace that he stole from me. I honestly felt defenseless.

It wasn't until one morning when I bowed down and simply said, "Please God," that I felt a shift. I was desperate. I had no other words but "please." And I felt God say in that moment, "It is yours, daughter." I had asked for peace, for joy, and for my mind to be at ease. He told me it IS yours. I felt such a peace overwhelm me in that moment that I couldn't help but cry harder. I didn't feel that heaviness that I had been carrying around.

I had found what I was missing. I had found what God was prompting me to "protect." My inner peace. The peace that only comes from the Holy Spirit. The peace that keeps us stable and able to rest in the midst of the craziness or trials in life. And once I found that peace, I had to protect it.

The best example that I have found of protecting your peace is found in 2 Chronicles 14. This text opens up introducing the next king in line to sit on the throne in the kingdom of Judah. However, let me give you some background first.

There was a point in history where the Israelites kept asking for a king, someone to rule over them (1 Samuel 8). God answered their requests and king Saul became the first king of Israel (1 Samuel 9). After Saul, came David, then Solomon, and then a series of kings followed. Many of the kings turned the people away from the Lord. They worshipped false gods and idols. They built images. They did things that were far from pleasing to the Lord.

Eventually the kingdoms split into the kingdom of Judah and the kingdom of Israel and each kingdom had a king. On both sides, many of the kings did wrong in the sight of the Lord. However, if you keep going through the history of the kings we eventually get to Asa, king of Judah.

The text in 2 Chronicles 14:2-6 begins,

"Asa did what was good and right in the eyes of the Lord his God. He removed the foreign altars and the high places, smashed the sacred stones and cut down the Asherah poles. He commanded Judah to seek the Lord, the God of their ancestors, and to obey his laws and commands. He removed the high places and incense altars in every town in Judah, and the kingdom was at peace under him. He built up the fortified cities of Judah, since the land was at peace. No one was at war with him during those years, for the Lord gave him rest."

What I have learned in my life is that our peace can be rocked, shaken, or tested at any moment. In fact, John 16:33 tells me so. "I have told you these things, so that in me you may have peace. In this world you will have trouble. But take heart! I have overcome the world." Just think about it. You can be having one of the best days ever but then someone who isn't having the best day, calls your job and curses you out. Or maybe you are driving, and someone cuts you off. Maybe you receive some bad news about a loved one or about yourself that you didn't expect. Maybe you have a big decision to make and you want to enjoy the transition, but you can't seem to. Or maybe you felt that your relationship or marriage was on a great track and all of a sudden, your partner decides to leave you. Your peace is being shook.

But what God showed me through king Asa is that if I protect my peace, it's harder for it to be shaken. Let's go back to the text.

While the land was at peace, Asa decided to build up towns and put walls around them with gates and bars. In other words, he built up his defenses. He was strategic and used that time to build. He didn't just settle and let down his guard because they were experiencing peace. He continued to protect it. As my study Bible put it, "king Asa recognized the period of peace as the right time to build his defenses--the moment of attack would be too late."

This is protecting your peace.

We must recognize that we are only safe when we take heart in the Lord. We just read John 16:33 which says to take heart because He has overcome the world. Not only that but it says that He tells us these things so that in Him we may have peace.

There are things in life that we just can't predict. We don't see that darkness coming, we may not see that break-up coming, or we may not foresee that report from the doctor, yet when we can find our peace in the Lord, it makes those tough moments in life much easier if we constantly allow ourselves to trust God and hold on to His promises.

I had to make this decision one day when I fled down the interstate bent over in my car trying to make it to the hospital.

One night, I woke up in the middle of the night with sharp pains in my side. It was probably about 3:00 am and I had to be ready to leave for work by 7:45 am. I couldn't go back to sleep. I spent most of the early morning on Google trying to diagnose my symptoms. I had concluded that I either had appendicitis or a stomach ulcer.

Eventually the pain subsided midday while I was still at home in bed. Night came again and this time I woke up at 1:00 am. I grabbed my phone, went back to Google to try to see what home remedies there were. I had been a pretty healthy person with an occasional visit to Urgent Care, but I didn't feel that it was necessary to make a trip. Finally, the pain went away again but then it came back again. Within the next couple of days, I made visits to Urgent Care, the ER, a doctor, a gynecologist, and back to the ER. No one that I saw was able to tell me why I was waking up in the middle of the night with sharp pains. Their scans, tests, and labs all came back negative for what they believed it could have been.

Again, the pain subsided so I went in to work on that Friday. I was completely fine the whole day and then at 4:00 pm, thirty minutes before I left work, the pain returned at full force this time. When 4:30 pm came, I darted out the door and drove to the ER (a 30-minute drive from where I work). I called my parents to let them know that I was going to the hospital and they hopped in their car as. They were about three hours away but still made sure they came to be with me.

Once I arrived at the hospital, I could hardly walk. I hunched over as I walked in the ER and could barely get a word out because of how much pain I was in. The generous ladies at the desk took care of me and somehow understood exactly what I was saying. They got me checked in and I waited for a nurse to escort me to a room. I don't really know what was running through my mind other than *make it stop!* I was terrified.

Once I was in the back, I had a second CT scan and they still did not see anything, however, they believed that it was appendicitis. As my pain continued to increase and the answers were nonexistent, they called a surgeon and asked her to come to the hospital. She drove three hours to get to me. At this point, I was completely hunched over and could not stand up straight. It hurt to use the bathroom. It hurt to walk.

It hurt to move. They asked me if I wanted medicine and I said yes, however, even the strongest medicine did not do anything for the pain. I laid in that hospital bed waiting for answers. Thank God I wasn't alone though. Two of my good friends came to be with me, my parents arrived, and then the surgeon.

The surgeon came in, read over all of the notes, and asked if I wanted surgery or if I wanted an antibiotic. Without hesitation, I opted for the surgery, although I had no inkling of what was causing the pain. This is a rare case where naming the pain couldn't help me. (Refer to Chapter 2.)

I just needed the pain to cease, and by this time, I knew medicine wasn't going to suffice. It was a risky move, but I held onto my peace and God's promises. I knew that God wasn't done with me. I knew that He had told me that He still had things in store for me. I knew that this was just a hiccup in my journey and that He was going to bring me out of that surgery alive and well. I knew Peace and I had peace.

As a Christian, you aren't exempt from trials or pain in life whether it's physical, emotional, or spiritual, but God does promise to draw near to us if we draw near to Him (James 4:8). Not only this, He promises us that, "though the mountains be shaken and the hills be removed, yet my unfailing love for you will not be shaken nor my covenant of peace be removed." (Isaiah 54:10) To me this means that even when things in this life fade away or are shaken and stirred, His love and peace remains. Oh, and if you're wondering, my surgery went well, and it turned out that it wasn't an appendicitis after all. They believed it was a cyst rupture.

I protected my peace, and that was the only way that I got over that hiccup.

Now that we have talked a little about what it means to protect your peace, I also want to provide you with a list of things that I did in order to build my defenses and protect my peace.

Building Your Defenses

Surely, I didn't build walls or towns and gates like king Asa. However, I did find that there are simple tasks that were beneficial in building my defenses.

In the Chronicles text, Asa was fighting physical people and enemies. Our fight is a little bit different or at least the one I'm talking about is different. I'm talking about the fight against spiritual forces and darkness (Ephesians 6:12).

Now remember, protecting your peace is twofold. It is about seeking the Lord's peace, but it is also about maintaining that peace. Once you ask the Lord for peace and invite Him into your various situations, the tasks of keeping that peace become important. And like I said, we cannot control everything that happens, but we can control what we expose ourselves to, and that is so important.

Simple tasks such as monitoring what you are doing, looking at, or who you are with constantly will help you protect your peace. If you know that it is a trigger for you, why do that and threaten your peace?

You know better than anyone what things are your triggers. Maybe you don't know your triggers yet. Well, I encourage you to pay attention to yourself just like we did when we asked the hard questions in chapter 4. Pay attention to the shifts in your moods and the things that tamper with your mood. Pay attention to your mood when you watch certain shows or after certain events in your life. One thing my counselor encouraged me to do was keep a feeling journal. Doing so helped me identify what things in my life were threats to my peace.

Wrapping it Up

Transforming your mind is going to be important as you walk out of the mud and mire of life. Your mind and its thoughts play a huge factor in identifying how you see your circumstances and view your world. Know that you have the power to take charge and change those views.

Protecting your peace is a significant part of transforming your mind. When you don't have peace, it will affect you and those around you as well.

My challenge to you is to ask God to restore your peace if you recognize that you don't feel like you have peace or feel anxious, powerless, weak, or out of control.

Maybe you recognize that you need to protect your peace. I challenge you to build up your defenses by knowing your triggers and what environments and people tamper with your mood. And lastly, I challenge you to lean on His promises. I challenge you to replace the wrong thoughts with the right thoughts.

A transformed mind is just one tool to add to your toolbelt in the lifting process. And there's more.

Chapter 9

Community

Let me just get this off my chest before I change my mind. *You need people in your life.* Need. It's not an option or advice, it's the pure truth. You need people in your life.

I go back and forth with this a lot. Community is tricky. Relationships, whether friendly or romantic, are tricky. Today is a good day for me. Today I know I need community. Earlier this week, I probably would've said *No, I'm good, God is all I need.* Who knows what I'll think tomorrow or by the time you're reading this book.

I promised to be honest in this book. And the truth is, I change my mind about community daily. I'm probably the last person on earth who should be trying to teach you about community and why you need it and why it's so good for you. And also how it's great for accountability, encouragement, and support, among many other things. As you've probably seen and will continue to see in these last pages, God is working on my heart still.

There are days where I know I need community and how important it is, then there are other days when I am convinced that I am better off alone. Let's stick to the better side of this coin, or as I call it, "why not community?"

Why Not Community?

Friends, I think that there are a lot of answers to this question that may vary across age, race and ethnicity, gender, and maybe even culture. But one answer to this question that I have found to be universal is hurt.

I think it's safe to assume that we all have experienced hurt in our lives. Whether that be from a father that walked out or never showed up, a mother who abandoned you or never listened, a boyfriend or girlfriend who walked away, a friend who betrayed your trust, or someone who did something harmful, we have all experienced people hurt. If we are honest, we have all caused other people to hurt. And for some of us, that hurt can drive us the furthest distance from community.

I won't assume this is true of everyone because I know there are some of you tough-skinned people out there who may not be affected by those who hurt you. However, in my case, people hurt was the very thing that drove me in the opposite direction of community.

As a child, I always had a group of friends. Always. Middle school I had different "crews." High school I had different "crews." In college I had a group of friends. I always had people in my life. People I loved, genuinely cared for, and had some pretty amazing times with. But somewhere down the line many of those relationships vanished.

Friendships that I felt were solid fell off. Those I felt I really knew just disappeared. They all fell off for various reasons, some of which I know and others I don't have the slightest idea, but the thing is, it sucks losing friends. It sucks getting used to a life without someone you've been so close to for so long. You may have been lied to, felt neglected, betrayed, or written off, or maybe someone cheated on you in a romantic relationship. Regardless of what it may be, we have all experienced some type of hurt in our relationships. And that hurt can make a huge impact on our lives. It's an impact that can scar us, cripple us, and make us afraid to be in relationships again.

For me, all of the hurt and loss I experienced over the years stripped away any desire that I had of making friends or being in community. I missed the days of my youth where friendships weren't that complicated.

I was tired of being hurt by people. I was tired of hurting people. I was tired of trying to please people and meet their expectations. I was tired. I remember sitting in church one evening during my college years and the message was about community and why we needed it. God began tugging on some heart strings, but I wasn't having it. I remember the inner dialogue I had: *Not me. I don't need community. I'm good, all I need is God. People continue to let me down. I always have to reach out to people. I always let people into my life and then it fades. I disappoint people. They disappoint me. Yes, I'd rather just have God.*

This kind of thinking was futile for me. I would rehearse and believe those things so much so that eventually, I started to act heavily on them. I began to isolate myself and keep people at a safe distance.

I would sit in my room many days and nights intentionally isolating myself from the world. I thought that if I just confined myself to my room, I would avoid all pain. It could just be me and God and Netflix®, and I would be fine. I thought that it was safer to just be alone. I made a pact with myself that I would never let any other people into my life, and I went from being the one who never wanted to be alone to always wanting to be alone. I was hurt. I didn't know who I could trust anymore, and I didn't understand how friendships could go from thriving to dying overnight.

I recall times post-college where I sat in my room isolating myself from everyone and everything. I knew I needed people, but I didn't seek them out. I considered who I could call and reach out to but with every person I thought of that I could reach out to, I talked myself out of it. I told myself that this person couldn't help me or this person wouldn't care or this person wouldn't be able to feel and understand all that I was feeling. The excuses came one after the other. They were all things that I had conjured up in my mind to keep me from reaching out to the community that I had. Instead, I mastered the skill of isolation.

And if that isn't enough, let me tell you about the most recent example. Here I am at 24 years old, and I have still been keeping people at a safe distance and isolating myself. I didn't know that I was still doing it. Of course, God didn't shy away from calling me out and pulling on some heartstrings again. (As a quick caveat, let me just say that it is so challenging to write about something when you are still wrestling with it at the exact moment that you are trying to convince others that they need it. So, I'm talking to myself here too.) But I honestly thought I had dealt with my distaste for community a while ago, and I had let people in since then. But God revealed to me that yes, I had let people in, but not to the extent that He needed me to. I still had some wounds that I had bandaged but weren't completely healed. I put bandaids on what required stitches.

One night I was sitting on my couch watching TV as I ate dinner. It was about 5:30 pm and I knew that I had a Christmas party to be at by 6:00 pm. As time creeped closer and closer to 6 o'clock, I grew more comfortable sitting on my couch. Part of me wanted to go but the other part of me reasoned that I hadn't had any downtime that weekend and I just wanted to relax. I spent the weekend at a retreat, and I was around people way longer than normal, so I needed time to recuperate. Any introverts with me on this?

Well, I sat there on my couch and before I knew it, it was 6:30 pm. I decided not to go and just kept watching TV. About five minutes later, I received a text message from a friend inviting me to hangout. But I declined her offer too. The kind observation that my sweet friend shared with me knocked me into a night of reflection. There was no more relaxation for me. Her text shocked me. It cut me to the core. I was so convicted by her words. Maybe angry more than anything, but after I got over the anger, the conviction sank in.

She told me that I talk a lot about being in community but how I've never accepted an invitation when she has reached out. *Ouch, my friends. Ouch.* I knew she was right, hence my anger.

For my iPhone friends, in my pettiness, I gave the message a thumbs up and then turned my phone off. I sat there and really thought about what she said. I didn't want to respond right away because it would've been in anger. Instead, I cried. I cried, threw some things that were close to me, and then cried harder. (Don't worry, like I said before, God is still working on me. And I didn't break anything.) After I cried, I turned my phone back on and responded to her. I let her know that she was right. I did have a problem with community and was trying to figure out what it was.

Instead of having a pity party, I went into my room, sat on the floor, turned on some worship music, and grabbed a half-sized piece of paper and a sharpie. At the top of that paper I wrote "What keeps me from being in community?" And so, the work began. On that sheet, I jotted down any and every reason that I knew of that was keeping me from community. The Lord brought to my mind specific incidents and moments that were particularly challenging, and while I won't go into those details, these were moments that skewed my perspective of community and the need for it. They were moments that I had no idea were impacting my life even years after they occurred.

Leaving that quiet time, I had puffy eyes, a headache, and I was more exhausted than I was earlier that evening. But I also left with a greater understanding of why I was so opposed to community even though I wasn't aware of it.

Taking that time to really sit with the idea of community was so helpful and something that I truly needed. It's something that I will continually have to surrender to God but that is okay. The truth that I walked away with in that time was that no matter how much I want to not want community or how fearful I may be of it at times, I need community in my life. And if you find that you, too, may be wrestling with the idea of community and inviting new people into your life, I just encourage you to open yourself up to it. Yes, you may be hurt again, but the benefits of community greatly exceed any benefit that you may think you get from being alone and in isolation.

But before we get there, I must share what can happen when we operate outside of community.

Out of Bounds

In basketball, when you are holding the ball and step out of bounds, the possession gets turned over to the other team. We are going to use this analogy to illustrate how when we operate outside of community, when we step outside of the bounds of community, we give way for the enemy to gain possession of the ball, or in other words, our life.

In case you need another reminder, the enemy is looking to steal, kill, and destroy (John 10:10). Think of him like a stalker if that helps. That's a creepy visual, but he's really watching you. He may be invisible, but he is real. He is watching your every move, waiting for his chance. He is waiting to gain possession in the ball game of your life.

Now I don't say this to pressure you, but I say it to increase your awareness of the imminent danger that we are in every single day of our lives.

When we step out of the bounds of community, it is the perfect opportunity for the enemy to dunk on you. And to be dunked on is so embarrassing. It's also pretty funny to me.

But I have realized that in the past when I had stepped out of the bounds of community, it was the exact moment when my mind was flooded with thoughts of suicide and curiosity of how life would be without me. It was the exact moment that I questioned my purpose here on earth. It was the exact moment that he began to strip away my hope, identity, and purpose. I had allowed the enemy to torture me and whisper lies to me when I stepped out of bounds. I had allowed him to convince me that I was defeated when I stepped out of bounds. I allowed him to convince me that darkness was winning the game by a long shot, time was running out, and it was impossible to catch up.

This is what he does when you step out of bounds. He has no regard for you or your life. He couldn't care less about you. And it makes me so angry even sitting here typing this, because I could never imagine how someone could have so much hate that they look at another human being like they are nothing. I know it happens even today, but all that hate has to be exhausting. I've been angry, upset, or mad at people but not hate. That's an entirely different level that I hope to never experience.

But the enemies' hate towards me was so powerful that I grew burdened. I tried and I tried and I tried to fight back. Each day I fought. But with every shot I missed and with every step I traveled (not literally, still using basketball terms here), I failed. Because I was fighting alone. Alone and defeated.

You can choose to stay out of bounds the rest of your life. You can choose to keep hiding and holding in your problems. You can choose to live a miserable, lonely life that feels "safer" like I did for so long. But the only thing that you will find by doing so is defeat.

I can guarantee that. I can guarantee that because even in the beginning, in Genesis, scripture records that "it was not good for man to be alone."

Now this scripture is often used in the context of marriage but if you think about it in the context of relationships at large, God did not desire for Adam to live alone. Sure, he had animal friends, but that wasn't enough. God decided to place another human being in his life; a woman (Genesis 2:18). So, no, you were not designed to be alone.

Say these aloud with me:
I was not designed to live my life alone.
It is not good for me to be alone.
I will not live my life alone.

Say these declarations aloud daily. Write them on your mirrors or post-it notes. You are talking to the expert of isolation. It is so, so easy to run away from people and community when you have been hurt. It is so easy to build walls, shut doors, and keep everyone at bay. It's the easy thing, but what's easy isn't always good for us. Living alone, fighting alone, playing this game of life alone is easy, but don't you know that you have a whole team waiting to be tagged into the game? Don't you know that basketball is not a one-man game?

Typically, if a player has the ball and they are close to stepping out of bounds, you will see them quickly throw the ball to their teammate so they don't lose possession of the ball. Well, you have a whole team waiting with hands open to receive the ball. You have teammates all around the world that want to keep you in bounds. Maybe you haven't met any of them yet. That's okay, I believe that God can bring them to you. I believe that God will bring godly men and women to you, to help keep you in bounds. I pray even now as you read these words that God would begin to open doors for you to find these people. I pray that you would find a church family, a people that has your best interest at heart.

Again, I know it's scary. However, if you are going to transcend the darkness and fight the enemy's attacks well, community is necessary.

I'll end this section with this, because it needs to be said: we are all human. We all make mistakes. We are all broken people with damaged lives, experiences, or encounters that have shaped our worldview. We have experienced things that impact how we treat people, what we expect from people, and what we need in our relationships. We hold people to expectations that they could never meet. We are selfish, prideful, imperfect people. You are not exempt from that and neither am I. You are imperfect and broken. I am imperfect and broken. You will hurt people. People will hurt you.

I won't say that it will be easy to invite new people into your life. But I will say that as I remind myself daily of our humanness, our imperfections, and our brokenness, I am able to see myself and other people the way God sees us. As I remind myself of the enemy's pursuit and our original design, I am able to see that stepping out of bounds is just too risky. And with these things in mind, the more willing I am to stop playing a one-woman game and work with my team. *I will not live my life alone.*

Feel free to take a few moments if you need it. I know I need a second because that was a lot.

...

...

Alright, halftime is over.

I've talked about why we sometimes don't do community and what can happen when we don't do community, so now let's jump back in to the second half of the game. We are going to look at all the great things that can come from actually embracing community. Or in other words, "why community?"

Why Community?

The first answer to "why community" can be seen by talking about Maryland — the seventh state to join the United States.

I told myself that I had to dedicate a portion of this chapter to Maryland because it was driving in Maryland that reminded me of some very insightful things about community. And before you Marylanders get too excited, you may not enjoy what I have to say, but I do hope that my lovely commentary teaches you a little bit about driving.

After graduating from college, I was hired as a full-time admissions counselor at a local university. As a college admissions counselor, one of the duties involves traveling to different states and cities. Well, my territory was usually the Carolinas and a portion of Virginia. However, there was one week that I was asked to cover in Maryland in place of my coworker who could not travel. I didn't really have a choice, so reluctantly, I agreed.

I grew up in a city with about 100,000 people and have lived in a city with about 40,000 people for about six years. I am used to smaller cities. I enjoy two or three-lane interstates and minimal traffic. Imagine my surprise when the interstate went from two lanes to three lanes to six lanes the further north I drove. Cars seemed to magically appear from every direction. I was cruising, enjoying my pace, but suddenly cars began zooming past me. I am not a slow driver, or at least I don't think so, but I went five over the speed limit as I normally do, but that did not seem to be enough. I remember wondering to myself if there was some unstated, implied rule that you drive fifteen or twenty mph over the speed limit in Maryland. Seriously, I was confused. I had driven in Maryland before, but it was in more rural areas like Hagerstown, Maryland.

This time I was approaching Baltimore, Maryland, a city with a population six times larger than where I grew up. I'm sure driving in Baltimore is probably nothing compared to New York, New Jersey, or any other state or country like Germany, however, it was a lot for me. It was enough to teach me about myself, so let me just have my moment for those of you who may be reading and thinking that Baltimore is not even a big city.

The lesson I learned was on my way back home to Virginia. I had attended all of the fairs that I was scheduled to attend for the week in Maryland, and I survived, so I could return home. I was driving from the Eastern Shore back towards Baltimore, and again cars started zooming past me. I'm pretty sure the speed limit was sixty or sixty-five mph so of course, I abided by the law because I was not trying to return with a speeding ticket. However, a car almost running me off the road indicated that I needed to pick up the pace.

I increased my speed to about ten mph over the speed limit but the car behind me was still not pleased. This road bully (yes, I called them a road bully), would not budge so I continued to speed up. At this point, I'm sure I was going at least twenty mph over the speed limit because they just would not get from behind me. Exits passed and they did not get off, so in my mind I wondered why they refused to use any one of the other five lanes that were available to them. I was in the far right lane, the slow lane, so I felt like I was okay, you know? Not to this person. And they were plucking my last nerve.

One of my biggest pet peeves are cars who drive too close to my bumper, so imagine my joy in this moment. It was non-existent. (Many of the people in my life are convinced that I have road-rage, but it's really just a strong desire to be safe.) All I wanted was for that car to get over so I could continue living my life and cruise down the highway at the right speed, but they would not budge. It gives me anxiety when cars tailgate me, but I kept driving in my lane.

Eventually, the Lord sent an angel in the form of a while utility van that was going my pace. I positioned myself right behind this van and kept up with their speed. I kept a good distance from them, but I was able to drive comfortably again. And I'm pretty sure they were going slower than I was but I didn't care. At that point, the road bully had no choice but to get over because now he was up against two, not just me alone. And surely enough, he changed lanes. Hopefully, you can see where I am going with this, but in case you don't, my first point to "why community" is this: We are stronger, better, wiser, insert any positive adjective you'd like…together.

1. We are Better Together

We just talked about this previously with the basketball analogy. But to drive the point home, the

Bible tells us that two are better than one (Ecclesiastes 4:9). It tells us that though one may be overpowered, two can defend themselves (Ecclesiastes 4:12). It also tells us that it is good when God's people live together in unity (Psalm 133:1). The list could go on, but the crux that was illustrated to me with that white van is that life is not meant to be lived alone. I was reminded that in moments of pressure and discomfort, community can help me and support me in my times of need. I was reminded that community can help lift me up and help steady me when I feel that I am going to crumble.

This makes me think about Moses. If we look at Exodus 17, there was a moment where victory in a battle depended on Moses, but he could not do it alone. The Israelites had just crossed the Red Sea and watched their enemies get swallowed up by the waters (Exodus 14) but shortly after, they were under attack. A nation of Amalek called the Amalekites came and attacked the Israelites. Moses told Joshua to gather some men and go fight while he would go stand on the top of the hill with the staff of God in his hands (vs. 9). So, Joshua did as Moses said, while Moses, Aaron, and Hur made their way to the top of the hill.

The text states that as long as Moses held up his hands, the Israelites were winning, but whenever he lowered his hands, the Amalekites were winning (vs.11). To no surprise, eventually Moses' hands grew tired. The text goes on to explain how Aaron and Hur, the two men who went up the mountain with Moses, took a stone and put it under Moses so he could sit and they held his hands up (vs. 12). Aaron held one arm and Hur the other arm. Because of their help, because of the community that Moses had, he did not crumble. Instead, he saved an entire nation. Joshua and the Israelites overcame the Amalekites (vs. 13).

I believe that God intentionally sent those two men up with Moses because he knew that it was impossible for Moses to accomplish on his own. How long can someone hold up their arms alone? Moses was better with Aaron and Hur by his side.

My second point to "why community" can be found in the "bromance" of David and Jonathan, one of my favorite relationships in the Bible.

We all know the story or have heard about how David defeated Goliath right? Well, shortly after David defeats Goliath in 1 Samuel 17, we see the beginning of this bromance.

> "After David had finished talking with Saul, Jonathan became one in spirit with David, and he loved him as himself. From that day Saul kept David with him and did not let him return home to his family. And Jonathan made a covenant with David because he loved him as himself. Jonathan took off the robe he was wearing and gave it to David, along with his tunic, and even his sword, his bow and his belt" (1 Samuel 18:1-4).

I love their relationship because God was so strategic in the timing of their friendship. If we continue reading, as Jonathan grew to love David, king Saul grew to hate David. The Bible states: "

Whatever mission Saul sent him on, David was so successful that Saul gave him a high rank in the army. This pleased all the troops, and Saul's officers as well" (1 Samuel 18:5).

Saul didn't like this one bit because people began to acknowledge David's many successes while his were seen as minute. Saul eventually became obsessed with the idea of killing David. Jonathan, however, fought and pleaded with king Saul, his father, telling him that David has done no wrong. Did you catch that? Jonathan, David's close friend, is king Saul's son!

If we rewind to 1 Samuel 15, we learn that Saul disobeyed God and as a result it was said, "The Lord has torn the kingdom of Israel from you today and has given it to one of your neighbors—to one better than you." The kingdom was given to David. But what stands out to me is the fact that Jonathan acknowledges the calling on David's life, even though the throne should have been his since he was king Saul's son, according to customs. Jonathan says:
"Don't be afraid," he said. "My father Saul will not lay a hand on you. You will be king over Israel, and I will be second to you. Even my father Saul knows this" (1 Samuel 23:17).

As adamant as Saul was about killing David and shaming his name, Jonathan's loyalty did not change toward David. David had to flee for his life because of Saul's pursuit, yet Jonathan still encouraged, supported, and loved on David in a season that he needed it most. So, the second point is that community spurs you on.

2. Community Spurs You On

According to Webster's dictionary, to *spur* means to urge on or to incite to action. While David may have felt like his life was over, Jonathan stayed in his life and reminded him of his purpose. Jonathan helped David in whatever way that he could, to see God's promise for his life come to fruition.

This is the same kind of encouragement, support, and love that God offers us in the gift of community. And if you let Him, God can and will surround you with Jonathan's or Janet's in your life too.

In college, as I began to give up my ways and opposition to community, it wasn't long before God began to surround me with women who, just like me, were looking for community. I had prayed endlessly that He would surround me by godly community, and He heard my prayers.

I was reached out to about being a part of a small group of ladies that would meet weekly to read the Bible and to grow in relationship with one another. I believe our group was called "Pearls," but I can't actually remember what it stands for now.

Though I was a tough cookie to crack and wasn't necessarily an open book at first, I began to learn the value of community. I began to witness these ladies spurring me on and encouraging me to walk in purpose as a college student. I developed long lasting friendships with these ladies that I still have today. In fact, I had the privilege to be in two of their weddings. They were my Janet's. They are the women that would give me the clothes off their back without a doubt.

I could go on and on with examples about my life and how I found/find community to be beneficial, but I will stop here. Instead, I will encourage you to just read your Bible and see for yourself.

There is no perfect science to community, but you and I both need it, especially in our darkest nights. I hope I've at least convinced you of that. But if not, I'll let Jesus convince you. Because even Jesus invited His community to be with Him in His darkest night.

It was in the Garden of Gethsemane that Jesus sat and wept one night. He knew that men were about to come capture Him. He knew that He was about to face death. He knew what he was about to endure. Yet, he tells Peter, James, and John to come with Him (Mark 14:33). He told them, "My soul is consumed with sorrow to the point of death. Stay here and keep watch" (Mark 14:34). This is the same Jesus that rose from the dead. They may have fallen asleep instead of keeping watch but nonetheless they were there in His darkest hour.

And they weren't perfect people, but they were His people. They were His imperfect people that he walked through life with.

I don't know what life experiences may have shattered your view of people and community, but I do encourage you to explore it. I encourage you to sit at the feet of Jesus, put on your worship music, or do whatever you normally do when you spend time with Him and walk with Him through those experiences. We have all been hurt by people and likewise, we have all hurt people, so chances are that you, too, may be carrying around some people hurt that is impacting your relationships.

So, as I close this chapter, I invite you to explore your thoughts, ideas, perceptions, and feelings towards community. And if you recognize that you have been trying to fight this game of life on your own and have been failing miserably, I encourage you to invite other people to war with you. Whether that looks like going to church and asking for prayer or reaching out to one person that you trust, I urge you to share the burden with others and to let them help you carry it. This book is not intended to serve as a sufficient resource on its own. Yes, I am so, so grateful that you are reading this, however, in each chapter, if not every section, I will encourage you to action.

For this chapter, my action step is simple: if you don't have it already, pray for or get plugged into a community. Find some people who will be with you in your darkest nights. Find some people who will remind you that you are victorious in Christ Jesus. Find some people who will remind you of your worth and your identity. Find some people who will encourage you, rebuke you, intercede for you, love you, and accept you.

Your life depends on it.

And if you have community but haven't been operating in it, get plugged back into it.

Your life depends on it too.

Chapter 10

The Word of God

A pastor that I've heard speak many times always says, "Read your Bible every day. Read your Bible every day. Read your Bible every day." This may not be that significant of a statement to you by just reading it on paper. But if you were to hear the variations and inflections he would use at different points in the statement, you may have a different opinion. But it really struck me. At first, I wondered why he kept repeating the same phrase. But the point that he was trying to stress to us was that reading your Bible every day is something you need to do. No matter how many times he said it and how many different ways, he wanted us to know that our life depends on it.

Of all the tools that we have talked about so far, this discipline, along with prayer, is critical if we are going to ascend from the pits of life. The Bible is a great tool that we have access to. It is a resource, a manual, a guide, an instruction handbook, a compass, a map, and a GPS for life. Do you want me to go on?

The Bible has every single answer that we need. I know it doesn't often seem like it. I've searched far and wide for God to tell me what the best job is or where He wants me to go, but I don't seem to find those answers in the Bible. But what He does do is give me instruction through His Word.

In the fall of 2019, I started creating a handy dandy toolbox. This toolbox was a tiny $4.00 index card box that I picked up from Walmart. In this box, I placed packs of index cards along with find-it tabbed index cards. It was nothing fancy, but it was a system that I was creating, that I still use to this day. On each tab I include certain themes such as "being set apart," or "direction," or "suffering." On each white index card, I write down scripture that I find during my quiet time that is applicable to that specific category. Whenever I get discouraged, I flip right to that section and pull out that note card and speak that scripture over myself until I believe it. I rehearse it and recite it all day long.

This is a practice that I began back in my college days without even realizing it. Though it looked different then, if you ever came to my college apartment, the walls were decked with scriptures, sort of like how we decorate our Christmas trees with beautiful ornaments.

I had index cards taped to my wall, I had canvases of scripture, and I had pictures of scripture everywhere. However, the difference between now and then was that they beautifully adorned my wall rather than being placed in a tiny portable box I could carry with me. Sure, I saw them every day, but I wasn't studying the Word or reading the Bible like I needed. And because I wasn't reading the Bible like I needed, I found myself looking for the answers everywhere but the Bible. I found myself fussing and angry with God. *You aren't speaking to me God. You aren't here. Do you even care?*

You see, I had access to God the whole time. I had access to His Word. I had access to hear Him speak but I wasn't listening. I wasn't seeking Him. I wasn't trying to have a conversation with Him. I was so busy yelling at Him as if He was the enemy.

Now, if you were to yell and fuss at me, you better believe I will stop listening in one second. It is impossible to have a conversation with someone who is angry and set on getting their opinion across. That was me. And maybe it's you too. Maybe you realize that you have been so angry with the season you are in or your current circumstances that you haven't allowed room for God to speak to you. Maybe you have been searching for answers everywhere but the Word of God. Maybe you have been reading your Bible after all and it feels like nothing is changing. I don't know where you may find yourself, but my advice to you is to keep reading, every day.

If you are the person who has been so consumed with anger that you haven't allowed God room to speak, I encourage you to just take a step back, admit to God that you are angry with Him, and that you feel that He isn't speaking to you. He can handle the truth.

If you are the person who has been looking for answers that don't seem to be found anywhere, I encourage you to take a step back as well and crack open your Bible. That dusty thing that's been sitting on your bookshelf for months. Open the Bible app on your phone. It does not matter which method you prefer, just open it. I personally appreciate the hard copy Bible when I am having my quiet time.

If you are the person who has been reading your Bible but you feel like nothing is changing, I encourage you to keep reading your Bible. What I have learned is that no matter what I *feel*, even if it doesn't seem like my circumstances are changing, by reading the Bible every day, my mindset *will* change.

Have you ever heard the song Way Maker? If not, please do yourself a huge favor and go listen. There are many versions but one new version that has been circulating added a bridge to the song that has wrecked my whole life. It talks about how God is working even when we don't see it nor feel it.

A lot of times, we look for a feeling. We look for the tangible, evident changes in how we feel. We want the pain, the darkness, the heaviness, the shame, and the guilt to go away, and many times it won't go away immediately. But the moment you take your mind off the feelings you aren't a fan of and focus on reading the Word of God and truly spending time with Him, your life will begin to change. When you look for God and not a change in your feelings, your life will change.

I know how that sounds, and maybe it wasn't the answer that you were hoping for, but it is the truth. I've seen it happen. It happened to me. I've seen it happen to many people in my life.

The Bible is not meant to be a feel good resource but a tool to equip you, empower you, encourage you, teach you, and steer you as you fight your way through life. It's God's love letter to His people. It is His truth that you have access to, and quite frankly, it is silly not to use it. Just like not using your car signal is silly. But we will get to that soon...

I'll let the previous words and my thoughts be sort of an introduction to this chapter. While I did touch on a few nuggets about reading your Bible, what I really want to drive home in this chapter is several reasons why it is imperative and wise to read your Bible. I also want to talk about what the Bible is not. So, let's start there: the Bible is not cake.

Bible ≠ Cake

The Bible is not cake. *Got it.* On November 7, 2017, I stumbled upon a quote that said, "the Bible is meant to be bread for daily use, not cake for special occasions." It's funny because I remember the exact moment and location of where I was when I stumbled upon the quote on Pinterest®. I was sitting in my hotel room in Virginia Beach on the eighth floor, room 807. I'm just kidding. I don't actually remember what floor or room number, but I do recall that I had the worst view in the world. I was in the corner of the hotel, so my view was the other half of the hotel and the condos across the street. No water, no sun. Worst room ever.

After glancing over that quote, the guilt sank in. I'm not sure what exactly I was looking for on Pinterest® that may have been cake related, but I began to realize how guilty we are, how guilty I am of only reading the Word on "special occasions." I began to realize that my Bible was that "cake for special occasions." For months it would sit in the corner of my room or on my nightstand somewhere collecting dust. I didn't read my Bible every day. I guess I didn't really see a need for it as long as I was feeling good or feeling like I was in a great place in life, or as I like to call it, on a spiritual high.

The times when I felt frustrated, when I felt hopeless, when I felt like my life was in shambles, when I just wanted to give up, when everything in my life felt so out of whack, dark, sad, confusing, and painful...those are some examples of "special occasions." Those were the times where my Bible would come out.

Please don't mistake what I'm saying. BY ALL MEANS read your Bible when you're going through those difficult times, but what I'm also saying is that you should ALWAYS be reading the Bible not just when circumstances get hard.

Maybe you don't enjoy cake but steak. Maybe your Bible is that nice steak you get to treat yourself to every once in a while. Maybe ice cream Maybe your Bible is that large Dairy Queen® Blizzard® with extra Reese's and whipped cream that you treat yourself to. Clearly, I'm hungry at this moment, because both of those things are things that I treat myself to occasionally. Well maybe not a large blizzard, but I do get a medium sometimes.

But if I can have a moment of honesty or confession: there are times where I'm going through, and I'd much rather have ice cream than pick up my Bible. There are also times where I would rather sit on my couch, stuff my face, and watch Chicago Fire on Hulu®. I wish I wanted to pick up my Bible to read. I wish that my first instinct was to run, flee, and grab my Bible, but that's not always how it goes. Am I proud of this? Not the slightest. But thank God for grace.

Sometimes it is easier to seek out the quick comfort. It takes two minutes for me to hop in the car and drive to Dairy Queen®. It takes two seconds for me to turn on my TV and access Hulu® or Netflix®. I prefer quick and easy results, and I'm not really a fan of waiting for anything. It takes time for me to go grab my Bible, declutter my mind, and invite God into my space. It takes time to invite Him into my anxiety or my fogginess. It takes time. Time that I'm not always ready to invest.

But these special occasions are dangerous. They are deceiving, and I'm pretty sure that they hurt God too. I mean you'd be hurt if someone you considered a best friend or someone you loved only reached out to you when something was wrong or when they needed something. Right? I'm convinced that God feels the same way. And you may be thinking, well, He's the God of the entire universe. Does He *really* care about me not reading my Bible? Well, friends, the answer is yes. Yes, He does care because He cares about all of His sheep. This is demonstrated in Matthew 18 verses 12-14:

> "What do you think? If a man owns a hundred sheep, and one of them wanders away, will he not leave the ninety-nine on the hills and go to look for the one that wandered off? And if he finds it, truly I tell you, he is happier about that one sheep than about the ninety-nine that did not wander off. In the same way your Father in heaven is not willing that any of these little ones should perish."

God cares about the choices we make and the things we do or do not do. He is God. He is not a robot who is void of feelings and emotion. Our actions affect Him deeply.

Now I could go on a whole spiel about how hurt God was when the Israelites kept living void of

Him and His Word. Just reading the Bible will show you that. Whether it's the book of Jeremiah or Isaiah, it is evident that our actions can break God's heart. So, I honestly believe and reason that only reading our Word on special occasions is an action that breaks God's heart too.

No matter what your special occasion may be or what your quick comfort item may be, only you know how you treat the Word of God. So, let me ask you: is your Bible bread for daily use or cake for special occasions? If you find that your Bible has been more like that cake for special occasions, that is okay, there is grace. I don't say all this to make you feel bad or to make you feel like you are a horrible Christian, but I do say it to challenge you.

Our Bible isn't a resource that should be dusted off when needed. It is a manual for life. God told Joshua to keep this law on his lips always and to meditate on it night and day and by doing so he would be prosperous and successful (Joshua 1:8). His instructions were to keep it on his lips always. In every occasion. All the time. Regularly. Consistently. Repeatedly. In the same way, we should follow this command.

And I know that it won't be easy, because even today I sometimes struggle with it. I know that I should pick up the Bible. I know that I should run to Him. I want to run to Him and pick up the Bible. Yet, I don't always do this. Like I said, sometimes I search for the quick fix.

But what I have found and am finding today, is that the more I deny my desires for the quick fix and instead pick up my Bible, the more I fall in love with God, the more I fix my eyes on His promises, the more I make wise decisions, and the more I approach my circumstances with a positive mindset.

So, there we have it, friends: The Bible is not cake. We need the Bible every single day, not just on our worst day.

Now that we've briefly talked about what the Bible is not. I want to talk a little more in depth of why we should be reading the Bible every day.

I'm sure many of you reading this will be able to relate to this next example in some way, shape, or form. I'm going to talk about driving again.

Reason 1: It's Dangerous to NOT Read Your Bible

You may think that I am joking, but I believe that if I had to pick a side job, I would make an excellent drivers education teacher or a traffic officer. Before I changed the title of this section, it was called "My perfect side job."

In my years of driving, I've learned so many golden nuggets about life and living as a Christian. It's truly amazing how God can speak through seemingly mundane things when we open our eyes, ears, or hearts to it.

Now you have already heard me rant about cars that ride your tail and speed in a previous chapter, but now I want to talk about those of you special drivers that enjoy switching lanes or turning without a signal. I have a special place for you in my heart. It's pretty bad how annoyed I get when I see a car veering into my lane or into another lane without the simple flick of a turn signal. *You better not!* is what I say to the car as if they can hear me talking to them. It doesn't help, unfortunately. They still make their way into my lane void of a signal.

What I realized is that not using a signal is very similar to not reading your Bible every day. Hear me out. The turn signal is a safety feature designed to indicate and communicate with other drivers on the road. When you do not use your signal and instead decide to merge into a lane without warning, you place yourself and those in your path in a position that could potentially harm the both of you. According to the Society of Automotive Engineers, over 2 million accidents that occur in a year are attributed to failure to use turn signals. It is the leading cause of motor vehicle accidents in the U.S.

When we maneuver through life without using the very Word from the mouth of the Creator, the Word that is good for teaching, rebuking, correcting, directing, and so much more, we set ourselves up for an accident. God kindly rebuked me one day when I was driving. And don't you worry, it wasn't because I didn't signal, it was someone else who didn't.

One day when I was driving, I became really upset because a car made its way into my lane without a warning. *Seriously, why would you do that? Is it that hard to use your signal when it was designed to keep you and me safe?* Now, I'm pretty sure I didn't verbally say that last part, but it was probably a thought that passed through my mind. I had a whole dialogue as I often do in order to keep me from doing something irrational while driving.

I wasn't in danger or almost in an accident or anything when that car came into my lane, but I did have to slam on breaks. And what if there was a car following me? It would have smashed right into the back of me. Thank God this did not happen, but still, it's where my mind went.

What the Lord taught me in that moment was that so many of us wander through life doing the same thing. We don't use the safety feature and resource that can protect us, direct us, give us peace, hope, joy, or anything else we may need. Just like the driver who does not use their signal, when we are not using our Word and reading it daily, we can cause danger and open ourselves up to danger.

It's like struggling through thick fog and not using the special glasses you have to navigate and actually help you through it. (I'm not exactly sure if that's a real thing, but it was the first thing that came to my mind. I do know that firefighters have a thermal camera to see people through smoke.)

But if that doesn't work for you, then think about walking or driving somewhere and the sun is blinding you, and you have sunglasses within arms' reach, yet you don't use them.

My point is we have a resource to help us in any and every time of need in our lives, yet we don't even access it. And there are so many easy ways to access it. You can download a Bible app for free on your cell phone. You can google the Bible and specific scriptures for free. It is available whenever and wherever. Just as the turning signal is a safety feature to guide us every time we step into our car, the Bible is a safety feature to guide us along the pathways for our life. The Bible keeps you from disaster and disheveling your entire life.

Reason 2: The Bible Keeps You Reminded

The second reason I'd like to share to convince you that reading your Bible is important, is that it keeps you reminded.

The Bible is filled with thousands of promises for God's children. That's you and me. And it is these promises that can help keep us reminded of the truth, reminded and focused on the path of life, reminded and focused when it seems there is no way out, reminded and focused when despair haunts you, and reminded and focused when you're unsure if you want to see another day.

Had I not read Isaiah 26:3 when anxiety was wearing me down, I would have never known that God keeps those whose mind is focused on Him in perfect peace. Had I not read Isaiah 43:2 when I felt like I was walking through fire, I would have never known that the fire wouldn't take me out. Had I not read Proverbs 3:5-6 when I couldn't understand what God was doing in my life, I would have never known that He would direct my paths if only I would stop leaning on my own understanding. Had I not read Romans 8:1 when I was struggling with guilt and shame, I would have never known that there is no condemnation for those in Christ Jesus. Had I not read Psalm 121 when I was hopeless, I would have never known that I could find help and strength in the Lord.

I could go on and on filling the rest of the pages of this book with scriptures that have helped me navigate life, but the bottom line is that by reading the Bible we are reminded of truth and of God's promises. And we need that more than we know. Life is complicated and can be messy and hard and we can encounter some pretty terrible and painful things, but when we open up the Word and speak truth, life, love, peace, hope, and joy over ourselves, it *can* change things if we allow it.

I believe it was back in 2014 that I was introduced to Christian rap. At first, I was sort of opposed to it because it was just weird to me, but the more I listened, the more I grew accustomed to it. There is a song called *Promises* by Da' Truth featuring Isaac Carree. I'm not sure where I first heard the song but it popped up on my playlist as I am sitting here on my floor writing at this very moment, and the lyrics perfectly illustrate what I am going to say next. Paraphrasing the hook of this song, it says not to give up the fight even though things may not look good or feel good.

This song points out something very real: life will not always look or feel good. The Bible even tells us that in John 16:33 (NIV). It tells us that in this world we will have trouble. But we can take heart because He has overcome the world. The TPT version puts it like this: "For in this unbelieving world you will experience trouble and sorrows, but you must be courageous, for I have conquered the world." You *will* have trouble.

You and I are not exempt from trouble. The scripture just told us that. But trouble is temporary. Every day I need the reminder that what I see is temporary. Every day you need the reminder that what you see is temporary. And I'm not going to sit here and act like that's an easy thing to remember because I know what it feels like to struggle and not see a way out,, but what the scripture and the song tells us is that even when everything doesn't feel good or look good and trouble is knocking at the door, everything will be alright. It will be alright *because* He has overcome the world. We must hold on *because* He has overcome the world.

That may not give you a great bit of comfort right now, but if you hold on God's promise, knowing that everything will be alright because He has overcome the world, it gives you a different outlook. It can help keep you on the right path if you decide to believe it.

This is what the Bible is for. It is available to us, but it is our choice to believe what it says. It is our choice to believe that God can overcome our situation. It is our choice to believe that God is able to bring you through the storm. It is our choice to believe that God is with us in the fire.

I cannot make you believe that, but I do pray that your eyes would be opened to the truth and that as you read your Bible every day, you would find true comfort in His Words. I pray that His promises would keep you on the path and reminded of His goodness even when you can't see or feel it.

Reason 3: The Bible is Nourishment

The third reason that I have found that should prompt us to read our Bible every day is that it is nourishment.

When you eat good things, healthy things, how does your body feel? Now, when you eat junk food or fast food, how does your body feel? I would hope that you had two different answers to those questions. If you didn't, I'd be a little concerned. Just go a week of eating nothing but fast food and snacks. You'll see. But for me, I notice that when I am eating good things or things that are considered "healthy," I feel more energy and satisfied, whereas when I eat junk food, I often feel sluggish and tired. What I feed myself with oftentimes has an impact on the way I feel.

In the same way, what I feed my mind with has an impact on my outlook and perspective in life.

We talked about this briefly in the chapter titled "A Transformed Mind," and what you watch, what you listen to, and what you surround yourself with is what you will imitate in your everyday life. When you are feeding yourself with the Bible, you are fueled with energy to walk out and live your life as God intended you to. When you are feeding yourself with the Bible you are fueled with truth that can transform lives.

Did you know that bread is also used as a metaphor for the Word of God? As Rick Warren puts it, "bread is a symbol for the Bible, which is our spiritual food. When the children of Israel were walking to the Promised Land, God dropped manna from Heaven for the people to pick up because they had nothing to eat. God gave them this bread to teach them that people need more than bread for their life. Real life comes by feeding on every word of the Lord. You don't just need physical nourishment; you also need spiritual nourishment."

If you are not seeking spiritual nourishment daily, you will be spiritually dead. Sure, you may be fine physically, but eventually you will feel the repercussions of not being spiritually nourished. You place yourself at risk of walking around malnourished and unable to remember or walk in the promises of God. Not only this, but your malnourishment affects others too.

When I was in middle school, I drew a stick figure of a girl that had on a pink shirt that said *it's all about me*. I'm not sure if the school gave us this option or it was my parents, but I remember having a magnet and a white t-shirt with my drawing on it. I was convinced that life was all about me. Though it was cute and innocent then, it's not so cute and innocent as I am an adult.

What God constantly reminds me is that this life is not all about me. It's about Him and His glory. No one that God called in the Bible lived their life for themselves. Every experience and every truth they learned, they went out and shared with the people in the world. In the same way, our experiences and our journeys are not for ourselves. If I am not prayed up and nourished with the Word, it is going to be extremely challenging to go out into the world and do what God wants me to do. I'm not saying that it's impossible, but it may be tough.

I have realized that the days that I do not wake up and spend intentional time studying and reading the Bible, the more insufficient, powerless, and weak I feel. I'm not exaggerating. When I am in the presence of God and reading, soaking, and listening, I can love better, I am kinder, I am confident, I am joyful, I walk with purpose, I can think clearly, and I feel energized for the day. On the other hand, when I do not spend time reading the Bible, it is a recipe for disaster. I can be a complete grinch. I do not love well. I am easily irritated, I am snappy, and I'm distracted.

John 15:5 says, "I am the sprouting vine and you're my branches. As you live in union with me as your source, fruitfulness will stream from within you--but when you live separated from me you are powerless." If I might add or translate, you are malnourished when you live separated from God. You cannot bear fruit.

You are not just living for yourself but for others too. You are the vessel that God needs to use to reach the next person who is struggling with the very thing that you are in the process of overcoming. But if you are living apart from Him how can He do that? If you are living like I was, thinking that it is all about me, how can He use you?

He is our source and we need daily time in His Word if we are going to live a healthy, nourished life for ourselves and for others.

Reason 4: The Bible is How You Get to Know God

Though there are many reasons why you should read your Bible, I will end with this one: the Bible is how you get to know God. It is where you learn about His true character.

If there's one thing that I have learned about myself in my walk as a Christian, it's that I had many misconceptions about who God is. But through reading the Bible and seeing how God interacted with His people, seeing how Jesus operated in His relationships, and getting to know God for myself, I learned who He is and who He is not. In fact, I am still learning today.

It is through the Bible that we learn about God's true character. He is not this magical genie that we often mark Him up to be. He is a good, loving Father. He is a patient friend. He is a forgiving companion. He is a purposeful King.

There are many traits and things that I have learned about God, but the one that sticks out to me most and the one that helped me navigate the mud and mire was that He is purposeful.

A lot of times when life is in shambles and we can't see our way out, it's extremely difficult to believe that what we are going through serves a purpose. One day, I was having a conversation with my close friend and sis about how we both are going through what feels like the longest valley.

We both were in seasons of life where all we could do was just praise God that we were able to wake up and see another day. Our circumstances aren't really what we imagined to be dealing with in 2020. We thought 2020 was going to be our year, but it almost felt as if the attacks were close and often. We wished we could say that they were far and few but that wasn't the case. However, what held us was the fact that we know that nothing in our lives is purposeless. Whether our trial is a spiritual attack from the enemy, a gift from God to strengthen us, or a combination of both, we know that it serves a purpose far greater than what we could even imagine.

And this is the same truth that you must come to know about your current circumstances. As I've said many times in this book, I do not know what your struggle or circumstances may look like. However, one thing that I know to be true is that you will walk through and see the light on the other side of the battle if you just hold on. God is not a man that He should lie, and He will not leave you in the fire to be burned nor the waters to be drowned. He is with you and He is able. It is who He is, and He never leaves a sheep behind.

Conclusion

Friends, I encourage you to read your Bible every day. Whether you prefer to wake up early and get your reading in like me, or you prefer to read it during lunch, I urge you to carve out time in your day to sit and actually read the Word, study it, and apply it to your life. Your life depends on it, your nourishment depends on it, and most importantly, your relationship with God depends on it. And, friends, my hope is this: may we not forget on our best day that we still need God as desperately as we did on our worst day.

This is a discipline that is critical if you are going to press through the darkness and despair. It may not come easy, but it is the Word that helps light our path to freedom as we navigate darkness. We need it.

Chapter 11

Prayer

> "To be a Christian without prayer is no more possible than to be alive without breathing."
> –Martin Luther

I will never forget the first prayer that I learned. *God is great, God is good, let us thank Him for this food. By His hands we are fed, give us Lord this daily bread. Amen.*

My parents taught my brother and I to recite this prior to eating every meal to thank God that we have food to eat. Even if we didn't necessarily like what we were eating, we still thanked God.

Wouldn't it be great if we had that mindset with our problems? If we thanked God for our situations in life even if we didn't necessarily like what we were going through? I say yes, however, I have found that many of us today have been trained to wish away our problems, including me.

I've definitely had moments that I would pray, "God, please take this pain away. I won't do x, y, or z again." Then once the pain I felt was gone, I would turn back around and do x, y, or z. I was missing it. I had a misunderstanding of prayer back then.

So, let me ask you: what does prayer mean to you? What does prayer consist of to you?

Today, I would say that prayer is communication with God. It is an opportunity to get to know Him, to thank Him, and develop a relationship with Him. It is a privilege that you and I have as believers.

You may have come up with something similar to me or maybe your thoughts are completely different, either way, I do encourage you to spend some time thinking about how you personally view it.

Now that that has been established, my hope for this chapter is to show you some truths that I have found helpful about prayer. These are things that I previously had false beliefs about. The first is that prayer is only a means to present your needs to God and for Him to answer.

In actuality, prayer is so much more than that and I will show you that by introducing you to A.C.T.S., a helpful acrostic that helped me understand prayer in college. This method helped me to be purposeful when praying rather than only going to God with a list of things that I wanted or needed Him to do. As a result, I have been able to develop a meaningful relationship with Him that says, "I love You because of who You are, not just what You can do for me."

I began to incorporate these 4 elements when I spent my time with God, and I still try to do so to this very day.

This acrostic can be a reminder for the most devout Christian or for the new believer just learning about prayer or for anyone in between.

A.C.T.S.

A.C.T.S. stands for Adoration, Confession, Thanksgiving, and Supplication. Adoration is praising God. It is an act of worship that shows just how much you care for Him. Confession is admitting your shortcomings and sins and asking for and acknowledging that you need forgiveness. Thanksgiving is thanking God for what He has done in your life or what He is doing in your life. This could be as simple as thanking Him for waking you up this morning. Lastly is supplication. Supplication is when we present our requests to God, whether that be personal requests or requests of a friend, family member, child, spouse, coworker, or someone or something else.

This is not a model that absolutely has to be followed. However, it is a model that challenged me and allowed me to see that there was more to prayer than just asking for something. Prayer should be a conversation with God.

Now that I have broken down the elements of prayer, I'd like to bust a myth that you may believe or an act that you may participate in without recognizing it: only praying in the bad times. Instead, I'd like to show you that on this journey, prayer must happen continually. In the good and the bad. In the high moments and the low moments. Just like reading your Bible is not cake for special occasions, neither is prayer.

Pray Continually

In 1 Thessalonians 5:16-18 it says, "Rejoice always, pray continually, give thanks in all circumstances; for this is God's will for you in Christ Jesus" (NIV). Daniel 6 introduces us to a man named Daniel who demonstrates this perfectly in my opinion.

Daniel was favored by the king because of his exceptional qualities and was going to be elevated to a high office. However, Daniel was strongly despised by some of the administrators in the kingdom. Or in other words, he had some haters.

As I read about his life, I found that the administrators knew that the king favored Daniel and was going to set him over the entire kingdom but the administrators didn't want that to happen. They didn't want Daniel to have such a high position. so they plotted against him. They decided to attack the one thing that made him stand out from the rest: his relationship with the Lord.

The administrators went to the king and talked him into making a law that the people could not pray to any god or human unless it was to the king himself (Daniel 6:7). The law was passed stating that anyone who did not follow the decree would be thrown into the Lion's den. The Bible goes on to say, "Now when Daniel learned that the decree had been published, he went home to his upstairs room where the windows opened toward Jerusalem. Three times a day he got down on his knees and prayed, giving thanks to his God, just as he had done before" (vs. 10).

As we keep reading, we see that the men came to the king and reminded him that he could not go back on his word since the decree was published. Once they reminded him, they told him that Daniel was not obeying the decree. That's so dirty, right? They threw it in the king's face. And because the king favored Daniel so much, he was stressed. He couldn't go back on his word, so the king followed through with the decree and threw Daniel into the lion's den. If we keep reading it goes on to tell us:

> "A stone was brought and placed over the mouth of the den, and the king sealed it with his own signet ring and with the rings of his nobles, so that Daniel's situation might not be changed. Then the king returned to his palace and spent the night without eating and without any entertainment being brought to him. And he could not sleep. At the first light of dawn, the king got up and hurried to the lions' den. When he came near the den, he called to Daniel in an anguished voice, "Daniel, servant of the living God, has your God, whom you serve continually, been able to rescue you from the lions?" Daniel answered, "May the king live forever! My God sent his angel, and he shut the mouths of the lions. They have not hurt me, because I was found innocent in his sight. Nor have I ever done any wrong before you, Your Majesty." The king was overjoyed and gave orders to lift Daniel out of the den. And when Daniel was lifted from the den, no wound was found on him, because he had trusted in his God" (Daniel 6: 17- 23).

The people who were against Daniel wanted him to stay bound and die in that den. They brought a stone and placed it over the den to ensure it. But Daniel stayed true to God, while suffering, and God not only answered his prayers, but He also provided him a way out. The enemy wanted to take Daniel out. But through the power of prayer, Daniel was able to say that his God sent his angel and shut the mouths of the lions.

Daniel didn't just pray because he was going to be thrown in the lion's den. No, the Bible says that he "gave thanks to God, just as he had done before" (v. 10). This tells us here that praying was a pattern for Daniel. He did it three times a day, regardless of his circumstances.

Unlike Daniel, a mistake that I have made in my life is forgetting or rather not taking the time to pray daily. And the moment that I stopped praying consistently, I opened my mind up for the enemy to attack again. This happened in 2019.

2019

It was December 31, 2018, and I was feeling great about the upcoming year. *2019 is going to be a good year for me,* I thought. This has been partly true, however, it has also been one of the most challenging years I've had thus far. Every day for three months from February to April, it felt like I was walking around with a large weight crushing my insides. I was depressed, again. I was extremely anxious about everything. I was stressed with my graduate school classes. I was navigating my first relationship. Work was crazy. There was just a lot going on.

The depression was more extreme than it had ever been. I remember crying myself to sleep many nights or sleeping on my bedroom floor. I was laying in the dark during the weekends, isolating myself from the world, sulking, and not eating. I even went to the extreme of calling out of work because I didn't feel well. I felt so far from God again, and this time, it truly felt like He was nowhere to be found. However, the truth was, He was right there with me in that darkness. I had let the busyness of life pull me away from Him. A lot of things were going on in my life, and sadly, taking time to pray was just not at the top of my list.

It's a given that we will have many highs and lows in our life. And I am not saying that praying will keep all the lows away, but I am telling you that if prayer is something that you practice in all circumstances, you will know what to do when the darkness comes back. If prayer is already a pattern in your life, you will always be ready to pull that weapon out when the darkness or other things try to come at you.

Another golden nugget that I learned about prayer is that I have the ability to ask God the purpose for my pain through prayer.

The Purpose for Your Pain

I would not be where I am if I hadn't learned to look at my pain differently. In a worldly view, pain is thought of as bad and something that we want to avoid at all costs. However, if we consider it through a biblical lens, it is something that God can actually use for good.

Consider this note from author, singer, speaker, and founder of Hope For The Heart counseling ministry, June Hunt. June states in her July 2013 letter on *Trials*, "In both the Old and New Testaments, we find numerous references to the refining of gold and silver as a parallel of God's refining us through painful trials. This unforgettable allegory is meant to help us understand the purpose beyond our pain—to conform us to the character of Christ. Clearly, we don't develop Christlike character all at once. Character is forged over time, especially through fiery trials. Indeed, God is our Refiner." Psalm 66:10 says, "For you, God, tested us; you refined us like silver." I couldn't state this any better. Trials are meant to refine us!

Earlier in this chapter, I talked about a three-month period where I experienced depression and anxiety again. Eventually, I sought more help, and by the recommendation of a friend, I began seeing a Christian counselor.

After a couple sessions, I kept having dreams about fires. Unsure if there was a deeper meaning, I began to explain my dreams to her. I told her that in each dream a different building was on fire. That everything on the outside was crumbling but it seemed like the structure of the building stayed intact in each of the dreams. The buildings were completely demolished aside from the beams and foundation that formed it.

Soon after explaining, she brought everything into perspective. She believed that God had me in a season of refining. She told me that the buildings on fire were representative of me and the foundation that stayed intact was God. She explained that He was cleansing me of everything that wasn't like Him. He was refining me.

As I reflected, I could see that she was right. She then shared with me Isaiah 43:2 for encouragement. Isaiah 43:2 states, "When you pass through the waters, I will be with you; and when you pass through the rivers, they will not sweep over you. When you walk through the fire, you will not be burned; the flames will not set you ablaze."

She encouraged me to ask God to reveal the purpose for the pain instead of wishing it away. I realized in that time, that I was praying for relief and quick deliverance. I was attempting to shortcut God's process. And as my pastor said one Sunday, "A premature deliverance will cheapen God's process. God can deliver us at any moment in our different situations, however, God is not interested in changing our situation. He is interested in changing our character and developing us. He desires that we grow through our trials versus just going through them."

I can't even stress how true this is. Wouldn't you rather learn from a trial than just get through it only for it to come back around again? I know I would. I had to realize that God was using my pain for good, not to harm me. He wanted me to come out of that season of depression better than before. He wanted me to come out cleansed. But the only way He could do that was by keeping me in the fire rather than immediately pulling me out when I asked Him to. As the scripture states, "when you walk through the fire, you will not be burned; the flames will not set you ablaze" (Isaiah 43:2). This is the beauty of refinement.

With each high and low comes a meaningful lesson to learn, and if we ask God to show us what He needs us to learn, rather than pray our low moments away, we will gain wisdom to sustain us the next time adversity comes our way. We will find the purpose in our pain.

Prayer as a Weapon

I had to save the best for last. Prayer is the ultimate weapon that we have access to and must be willing to use in this journey. I'll be honest, for much of my walk with the Lord, I didn't take advantage of prayer. It was something that I never prioritized because in all honesty I just felt like I didn't have the time to pray. I'd make excuses and say things like *God knows my heart.* And, yes, it is true that He does know my heart, but how can I ever know Him if I am not taking the time to sit down and commune with Him? He knew my heart, but I didn't know His at all because I never spent time with Him.

I have grown such a love and passion for praying now that I am somewhat more mature in the faith. Prayer is an opportunity to intercede for yourself and for others. It is a way of aligning our thoughts and plans with the Creator of the Universe. It is a way to war in worship and fight every battle.

However, what I have found is that **in order for prayer to be used as a weapon, it has to be accompanied by faith.** It is easy to say a prayer if we take time to. But when we leave our prayer time, do we believe that the prayer has gone out and will be accomplished or do we believe that it hits the ceiling and won't happen?

The latter was my mindset for a long time. I didn't believe that God cared enough to listen to my prayers, and I didn't believe that He would really answer them. I lacked faith. And, sure, God can answer our prayers without our faith. However, I would ask what is the point of us doing something that we don't even believe in? What is the point of praying if we are not going to have faith for it to be done? Matthew 9:29 says, "You will have what your faith expects" (TPT).

This brings to mind the women with the issue of blood found in Luke 8. Jesus was surrounded by men and women. He was being asked to come heal a girl, but He could barely get through the crowd. There was a woman in that crowd who was ill and had a blood issue. And according to rules in that time, people who were deemed unclean were not supposed to leave their home. However, we find this woman in the crowd.

This woman finds the courage to reach out her hand and touch Jesus' garment thinking that if she just touches Him, she would be healed. She believed and so it happened. In that moment, Jesus looks around to find out who touched His garment. He finds the woman and says to her that her faith has healed her.

This woman essentially broke the law and was healed because she believed in what she was in need of.

Can you imagine what could happen if we possessed this same kind of faith when we prayed? As I type, I am just amazed and awestruck at this moment. I am even a bit challenged to pray bigger prayers. We have this access every waking moment. If we want healing, we must be willing to ask with an expectant heart to receive. If we want peace, we must be willing to ask with an expectant heart to receive it. If we are believing for a new car because ours is on the brink of death, we must be willing to ask with an expectant heart to receive it. God does not have requirements or restrictions for our prayers. In fact, part of James 4: 2-3 says, "you have not because you ask not" (NIV).

My encouragement to you is to use this weapon of prayer not only to present your requests to God, but also to worship Him, to get to know Him, and to fight this battle called life. God wants to know you, He wants to hear from you, and He wants to answer your prayers. But we must be willing to open our mouths and believe it.

And maybe you are someone who has prayed to God before and been disappointed because He didn't answer. I understand that completely because it has happened to me before as well. But one thing that I had to realize about God is that He is omniscient, which means that He is ALL knowing. Being that He is all knowing, He knows what is best for every single being on this earth. He knows when to answer "yes," when to answer "no," and when to answer "not right now." And that is exactly what He may do because He knows more than we do and what we need.

In His unconditional love for us, He would not answer a prayer that He knows will not benefit us. Sure, we may think we know what's best and what will benefit us, but in reality, we don't truly know what we need at all. Our duty is just to trust that He is God and knows what He is doing.

In closing, I want to emphasize that I am not saying that putting into practice the things discussed in this chapter will keep you from experiencing trials. No, on the contrary, I am saying that by praying continually, asking God to reveal the purpose for your pain, using your weapon, and incorporating the A.C.T.S. elements into your prayers, you will be equipped with a powerful tool that will help you in the mountaintop moments and in the low valleys; in the darkness and in the light.

There is so much more to prayer than I have shared. There is so much I want to say and show you and so much to learn and know about it. But I hope these few nuggets are enough to send you into your own excursion of learning deeper about prayer.

I encourage, even challenge you, to transform your prayer life starting NOW, by incorporating some

of the tools discussed in this chapter:
1. Try to incorporate the elements in the A.C.T.S. acrostic in your personal prayers.
2. Pray every day. Pray when you feel good AND when you feel absolutely horrible.
3. Ask God to reveal the purpose in your pain rather than wish it away.
4. Use your weapon of prayer and believe in what you are praying for.

Doing this won't be easy at first, especially if praying is not something you are accustomed to. It will take time and dedication. It will take setting aside intentional time to sit in God's presence to just have a conversation with Him. However, I really do pray that incorporating these nuggets will transform your life and your relationship with God like it did for me. As I practiced it every day, it soon became a habit, sort of like brushing my teeth. I didn't have to think about it; I just did it.

We have access to use prayer, and we would be remiss not to use it.

PART 4

Standing on Solid Ground
Walking in Freedom

...He set my feet on a rock
and gave me a firm place to stand.
Psalm 40:2 NIV

Chapter 12

A New Song

Wow, friends, here we are. We made it to part 4: the part of the book where we talk about standing on solid ground. This is the part where we get to talk about walking in freedom, so let's jump in.

If I were to ask you what is your favorite song, would you be able to answer? I'd say maybe half of you wouldn't be able to pinpoint one specific song. I fall in that half. But then the other half of you may be able to name one without hesitation. It's that one song that you play on repeat a million times and it just never gets old to you.

But how about if I were to ask you what was your favorite song in 2017. Or if I waited a few months and asked yet again, "what is your favorite song?" Chances are you'd have a different song in mind. The song that was once your favorite becomes a throwback song that typically only comes to mind when you hear it playing somewhere or someone says a phrase that triggers you to sing the song.

One Thursday evening, I was sitting in Starbucks® chatting with a friend and a song played and we both agreed that it used to be our song. Hours later, I couldn't remember what the song was; the memory of that sweet song came and went just like that.

There are thousands of songs released monthly, if not weekly, on so many different platforms. That's just my estimate, but I frequent Spotify® and YouTube® enough to see new songs released every day. With this many songs floating around, it's no wonder that our "once upon a time" favorite songs are pushed to the back of our mind and replaced so easily.

So, what's my point here? Just as your favorite song or songs from 2017 are replaced with this year's top hits, your song of despair, hopelessness, and pain can be replaced with a song of joy and freedom. Just like that. The song you once sang will become a distant memory. A memory that is never forgotten but replaced with a better song. A new song. But we will get to that shortly. First, we need to talk about life. Mostly my life. But we will look at yours too.

The Truth

What will you have me tell them God? "The truth."

Well, friends, there it is. God told me to tell you the truth, so here it goes. Life is hard. There, I said it.

The truth is that life is hard. It will not always feel like sunshine or rainbows, neither will it always feel like death and darkness. There may be days where you feel like you are on top of the world and can do anything, and there may be days where you feel like absolute trash. There may be days where you feel like everything is just going wrong and you can't breathe, and then there may be days where you feel so much joy, it feels like your heart is going to jump out of your chest. I've experienced many days. I've experienced the highs and I've experienced the lows. I've experienced the mountain tops and I've experienced the valleys. It's kind of like a roller coaster, only you are blindfolded and can't exactly see what's next.

I wish I could see what was next so I could prepare, myself but oftentimes that is not how it works.

Life changes daily. We may lose a family member. Someone may walk out of our lives. We may lose our job. We may fall out of love. Many of these things are unpredictable, many of these things won't make sense, and many of these things are hard. But, friends, no matter what valley we walk through in our lives, the feelings associated with the valley don't have to be our song. Pain, heartbreak, sadness, anger, fear, loneliness, abandonment, and whatever emotions that we may feel in our valleys do not have to be our song.

Music has been a part of my life since the beginning. When I was younger, I sang with the youth choir at my church. I'm not sure how old I was, but I know I had to only be 8 or 9 years old. Soon after I picked up an instrument. Well, not literally because that would be really interesting for a child to pick up a whole piano, but I started playing the piano. When I arrived progressed to middle school, I was a part of the chorus. I even recall my friend and I being the only two seventh graders making all district choir. In high school I was a part of the choir as well. I was part of show choir for a year. And today, I am a part of the worship team at my local church. Music is a very important part of my life.

As a sidebar, because I'm sure you'd love to know: if a day has gone by where I am not singing or humming or doing some kind of awkward dance or motion with my arms, skipping, or a combination of all three, something is seriously off.

My coworker friend pointed this out to me as I walked around the office in almost silence one day. She pointed out that I wasn't my normal self. I wasn't singing or bouncing around the office with a huge smile on my face. That is the quickest way to know that something is off or wrong with me. There's my fun fact for this chapter.

But I bring this all up because I have realized that music is universal. It is a way that we often express ourselves. Whether it's a song we have written or a song that someone else wrote and we resonate strongly with it, music can convey a message about us, to us, or to the world.

It's so versatile. There's different sounds, genres, styles, and instruments that all come together and can elicit different responses. At any moment, the right song can calm you, send you into deep worship, deep sadness, joy, or even start a praise break. Sometimes it helps you release anger. Sometimes it's useful for a nice cry. It has so many different forms that serve to get a point or message across.

Maybe you don't consider yourself the most musically inclined person? That's okay, I'm sure you still love or at least like music and singing. In my twenty-four years of life I have never met someone who doesn't.

So, I'm curious to know, what is the message that you are listening to? What song are you singing?

Maybe you are singing a song of joy and gladness. Well, praise God, keep singing that song! But I want to talk with those of us who may be singing a song of sadness or a song of hopelessness, despair, shame.

You may be asking yourself how do I know what song I'm singing. Well, the simple answer is to look at your life. Look at your patterns and how you think about things. What do they tell you?

By examining the song that I was singing, I realized that I was living in bondage. I realized that I was walking hopelessly, hoping for a brighter day, but expecting the worst. I didn't like the message that I was singing.

Waiting for the Other Shoe to Drop

I'm sure you've heard the popular idiom, "I'm just waiting for the other shoe to drop." People typically use this phrase after one event, when they are waiting for something else to happen, hence the dropping of the other shoe. It's usually not a positive event that one is waiting for either. It's typically something bad, like the expectation of something bad to happen or something to go horribly wrong.

The day that I realized that I was living my life like this, I was honestly pretty ashamed and terrified. I don't want to share this with you, but God instructed me to be honest, so I really don't have a choice here.

For weeks I had been struggling. I would wake up and feel depleted of energy. I wouldn't feel like doing anything, not even taking a shower sometimes. I had no energy to open my mouth and pray. No energy to open my Bible and read. I just felt blah. I felt just like the character Sadness in the animation film "Inside Out," before she discovered her importance. She was a blue character, literally. She walked around just trying to live her life, but often didn't understand why she was there. She was very monotone, often dragged her feet, and like I said before, blah. (This is a great movie by the way, so if you have not seen it, I highly recommend it. It stresses the importance of feeling all emotions, rather than just suppressing them in an attempt to always feel joy.)

Well, here's the part that I don't really want to share, but one morning I woke up, and I was still feeling the same.. I had requested off of work that day just to relax, and I also had a doctor's appointment. As I made my way to the doctor's office, I let out a brief sigh before walking into the office. I had been experiencing some abnormal pain and I wanted to be sure that it was nothing alarming. Walking toward the door, I thought, well today's the day the shoe is going to drop. Part of me hoped it would. I was already feeling bad, so I thought, *what's one more thing added going to do?*

And let me just say, I am very grateful and fortunate for the life that God has given me by grace, but sometimes, it feels too good to be true. Sometimes I am fearful to feel anything because I don't want it to be snatched away from me. Sometimes I'd rather just deal with the bad, ugly, and hard things of life, because I know what to expect. When things are going well and I feel good about life, I always anticipate something bad awaiting me around the corner. I know how this sounds but this is how I feel at times. I know how awful that seems, but it is the raw truth. I sometimes wait for the other shoe to drop. Sometimes I hope and pray for the best, but I expect the worse.

Again, I'll say, I am not proud of this, but I am human. You are human too. Maybe you resonate with me and realize that you, too, think in this way; join the crowd. We are not perfect human beings and we will never be. Our minds are jacked up, and our thoughts can be funky and shameful or dark. We have all experienced life events that have shaken us to the core. Events that have hurt us, hurt others, and made us afraid to live our lives. Events that have left us singing songs of hopelessness.

The song that I was singing was a song of hopelessness. The song that I am singing is a song of hopelessness. I have gone through the motions of every day just existing. Just breathing. Embracing every new day with the least amount of hope for a better day or for a new song.

I really don't want to live my life hopelessly, but it seems easier this way sometimes. I don't always want to do the work required to embrace the joy that I *could* have, because in an instant it could be taken away. So, what's the point?

Friends, I have embraced that there will be hard days. There will always be hard days. There will always be days when our feelings seem to overpower the truth of what we know to be true. And I wish I could tell you that you will always experience sunny days after your valleys, but I would be lying to you.

But what I can say is that as you continue to walk with God through your darkest valleys in life, He can and will transform your songs and your outlook on life. A life without sorrow and pain is a life that was not lived at all. In fact, our deepest pain and sorrow are the very things that make life meaningful. Our deepest pain and sorrow draw God close. Our deepest pain and sorrow teach us lessons that a diploma and multiple degrees could never teach us.

So, yes, the other shoe may drop in your life and bad things will happen. But we don't have to hopelessly wait for that shoe to drop. We don't *have* to sing that song. Instead we can embrace that things will happen because we live in a sin-infused world and trust that the God who created the heavens and the earth, is still in control and able to change the song we sing.

While I didn't initially realize it, I chose to sing a song of hopelessness because it was easier. I chose to sing that song because I didn't see the point of choosing joy when something bad was likely around the corner. But this song is a song of bondage, limitation, and complacency.

In Christ, we have a new song, friends. A forever song. In fact, we will have a whole playlist of new songs. They are songs that we will never and should never forget, and songs that will mark and indicate joy, peace, and new life.

New Joy, New Peace, New Life, New Song

"A new song for a new day rises up in me every time I think about how he breaks through for me! Ecstatic praise pours out of my mouth until everyone hears how God has set me free. Many will see his miracles; they'll stand in awe of God and fall in love with him!" (Psalm 40:3 TPT)

Can you guess who wrote this Psalm? I hope you get it right, or else I failed miserably in writing this book. Okay I'm exaggerating, but it's the man who has shaped the name and backdrop of this book, King David. It's okay if you didn't get it right, I forgive you. Let's just say that it's been a long day and you were too tired to think. I completely understand.

King David is the author. Let's not forget that this is the same David who was struggling and in desperate need of the Lord's help just verses prior. It's the same David who felt abandoned by God, attacked, and in despair (Psalm 13:1-2 TPT). The same David who felt like he was falling apart (Psalm 6:2 TPT). The same David who cried out constantly for the Lord to save him. Through everything that this man endured in his life, the pain, loss, rejection, abandonment, depression, and fear, his response was "ecstatic praise." He woke up every day with a new song for a new day of life.

Though I've never actually said the phrase aloud and I probably never will, one might say "how sway?" (And let me just say, I am not sure how or why that phrase popped up in my mind. In fact, I had to google what it meant and where it came from just to make sure it was appropriate to use.) In other words, you might ask, "how is it possible to face my circumstances and respond with ecstatic praise?"

I'm glad you asked, because years ago, I had the same question.

If someone looked me in the eye and told me that one day, I would look at my circumstances and respond with praise, I may have laughed at the person telling me. Or I may have mumbled something like, "yeah…okay" in the most sarcastic tone possible. I wouldn't have believed them. Honestly, I'm sure someone probably did try to tell me that years ago, but I couldn't believe it then.

And though I can't explicitly remember whether or not someone shared that with me, I do remember where I used to be and just how hard it was for me to believe that there was light on the other side of the darkness. It was one of those things that I saw other people discover, but I didn't believe it could happen for me. I didn't believe that I could see the light. And maybe you find yourself there too.

I remember a friend telling me once: *This is good and all Britt, but I just don't believe it for me. I don't see myself being able to come back from this.* If you do find yourself thinking similar to my friend, that is okay.

We all need some convincing sometimes. We all need or have needed tangible or visible evidence of things in different areas of our lives. So, hear me when I say, please do not beat yourself up about not being 100% sure that there is a brighter day on the other side of your storm. It's not always easy to just hear something and believe it right away. If that is one of your gifts, God bless you, but for me, I personally need to consistently see something in order to believe it.

I believe that this is exactly how David could so confidently show ecstatic praise. He witnessed God showing up time after time after time. Consistently.

The only way that myself and David can sing a new song is because we have seen God show up in our life. Consistently. When God shows up in your life at a moment that feels like you're staring death and darkness in the face, it changes you. When He whispers sweet truth to you at the point where you have decided you have had enough pain, it changes you. When you are running and feeling weary, broken, and exhausted, and He meets you, it changes you. When you can't hold on and can't fight anymore and He sends people your way, it changes you. When you realize the way that you were living could have killed you, and God made His way into your life, it changes you. An encounter with God changes you.

David went through some of the darkest times possible. He lost a child, he had a bounty on his head, his son sexually assaulted his daughter, he lost his best friend, and he was counted out by his own father. The list could go on, but David walked away with a testimony. A testimony that said,

> "I have seen you in the sanctuary and beheld your power and your glory. Because you love is better than life, my lips will glorify you. I will praise you as long as I live, and in your name I will lift up my hands. I will be fully satisfied as with the richest of foods; with singing lips my mouth will praise you" (Psalm 63:2-5 NIV).

I can't stress it enough, but an encounter with God will change you. You may be reading this and not believe me right now, but I just know that God will show up for you as He has done for me, for David, and many others.

Consider the song "What Mercy Did for Me" by a musical group called People & Songs. The gist of the song is that someone was lost and hopeless with death and darkness being the only song they could sing. But then the Lord found them, healed them, and set them free. My little summary won't do it justice but please consider taking a moment to listen.

One day, when I was sitting out on the porch of my office building during lunch, this song popped up on my YouTube® playlist. Immediately, I dropped everything and just listened. When the soloist began the song, something in me just paused. *I was hopeless too. I was lost too! Death and darkness were my songs too!* Lyric after lyric, I was drawn in. And it wasn't just by the words. It was her voice as well. I could feel that this wasn't just a song she was asked to lead but a personal testimony too.

Soloist after soloist, I could feel the personal testimony behind their words. And I have a very short fuse when it comes to crying, so in just seconds, the tears started flowing. I felt so much joy in that moment. I wanted to let out a scream, but you know that was not the most professional thing to do. Especially since just floors above me was the office of the President at the University that I worked in.

I concealed my scream at that moment, but internally it felt like my heart was leaping—like it was going to jump out my chest.

This, my friends, is the joy that you get to encounter when you wait out and endure the rough circumstances, dark moments, and difficulties. Before your eyes, God can turn your nightmare into a beautiful testimony. Before your eyes, He will replace your song of despair with a new song of hope. An encounter with God will change you. You will be compelled to sing, even if you've never sang in your life. Even if you are the most tone-death person alive, you, too, won't be able to contain your worship to God. (Just make sure you aren't too loud cause you may throw off those singing along with you. *Just kidding, I think.*)

I'm slightly kidding, but this brings to mind a memory from church one day. I can't really remember the song that the worship team was singing but I knew it was ministering to me. The tears were flowing, my hands were lifted, and it was as if it was just me and Jesus in that moment. However, a person behind me must have been hit by the Spirit because she burst out singing the song. She was completely off key, but God was doing something in her heart because the way she was singing. I just knew that He was in the process of rewriting her song. All I could do was pause in that moment, and I began to pray for that woman and what God was doing in her heart. Looking back, it is funny to me because I her singing caught me off guard.

If God has done something in your life, don't be ashamed to praise Him. When I started going to my current church, I was thrown off when I saw people run around the church, cry, dance, bow, and scream. But after a personal encounter with God, I understood.

And if you haven't experienced it yet, just wait. When God shows up at a time you needed Him most, you won't be able to contain your praise. You won't be able to contain your song. Don't contain your song. I don't care who may be around you, beside you, or behind you, do not be afraid or ashamed to sing that song.

Now I don't really want to change the topic and mess up this great, amazing, and life-changing news that I am sharing with you. But remember I said earlier that life is not all rainbows and sunshine. And also remember how we talked about how satan is out to get you and wants your life.

Well, I'd be negligent if I didn't warn you that he doesn't stop just because you have this new song. In fact, he may be more pressed than he was before to take you out.

I know, I know, this isn't the news you were hoping for, but we will get back to the happy ending that you *can* have shortly. But for now, let's talk about this copywriting con artist.

The Copywriting Con Artist

I know what you're thinking: that was a bit aggressive. I agree with you, but the nickname was just too good not to be used. It fits so perfectly in the context of this chapter. *The copywriting con artist.* Now, I do not endorse name calling or bullying by any means, but let's just go with it for the sake of getting my point across.

The bottom line here is that satan wants to steal your new song. The last thing that he wants to see is you walking confidently, victoriously, hopeful, and full of joy.

He's always whispering in your ear: "You'll never be free. You will always struggle with that. You're unlovable. God doesn't care about you. They hate you. You won't be understood. No one cares. No one will believe you. You can't possibly do that. You sound silly. You always mess up. It's your fault. You ruin things. You're wishy washy. God's clearly not listening to you. You could never…"

Who could possibly be joyful and hopeful when those things are constantly on the forefront of your mind and thrown in your face every time you try to progress in different areas of your life? You are reminded of a fabricated, convoluted truth with every step you take and everywhere you go. That's what satan does and what he will constantly try to do. He knows your story. He knows what happened to you. He knows your areas of weakness. He knows what tracks and memories to play on repeat to try to disarm you and leave you feeling defeated.

And if he can do that, then of course you won't sing a new song. You won't wake up feeling like God's mercies are new every morning. You won't wake up feeling like rejoicing because everything that satan has told you seems real. There's evidence that makes you entertain the thoughts. *Maybe it is true that I'm unlovable.* Before you know it, your mind is on this rabbit trail, lost in his web of lies. I'm sure you can resonate with this. I'm sure that it has happened to you at least once.

This is the effect that satan can have on you *if* you let him. This, is how he *can* steal your newfound song of joy. He creates a narrative that feels like it is absolute truth, gives you evidence to suggest that it is real, and then publishes it in the library of your mind.

And let's be honest, our mind is not the easiest place to navigate. In fact, our minds are in desperate need of some TLC. I believe this is why God instructs us to be transformed by the renewing of our minds (Romans 12:2).

According to Strong's Concordance, the Greek word for "renew" in the context of Romans 12:2 is "anakainōsis" (G342) which means, "a renewal, renovation, complete change for the better." "Renewing the mind is the adjustment of moral and spiritual vision and thinking to the mind of God."

So, what do you do? You weed out the narratives that aren't true. Just like you get rid of old clothes that no longer fit or you rid your Spotify® playlist of the old, ratchet music you use to turn up to before you were a born again Christian (*Yes I went there.*), you need to look at your mind and make sure the narrative that you are singing and living is the narrative that God has for you.

Jesus, of course, demonstrates this perfectly. In Matthew 4, we see that Jesus was led by the Holy Spirit into the wilderness to be tempted by the devil (v.1). After Jesus had been fasting and hungry, satan came at him with all kinds of things attempting to distort and disarm Him from the narrative that God had for him. No surprise here, but Jesus did not give in because He knew the narrative that he was singing. He did not give into the fabricated narrative that the enemy presented to Him. Jesus continued to sing His song.

So, sure, the enemy might be a copyrighting con artist who attempts to steal, destroy, or rewrite your song, but you have the ultimate song writer living within you— the song writer who did not allow the enemy to steal his song, and who has the ability to turn your sadness into joy, your pain into passion, your trial into triumph, and your grief into rejoicing.

I told you that I would get back to the good news. In Christ there is always a happy ending.

It's not like one of those cliffhangers or sad endings from a Netflix® movie that make you angry. One movie is coming to my mind specifically at this moment, and I think that I may still be slightly angry. It was such an amazing movie that my friend and I were watching one night on Netflix®, and it ended the worst way possible. We both were so drawn in and then the screen went black. I remember she and I yelling at the TV, "No, no, no." But to our surprise, the credits began to appear. The last scene was the two main characters in a car racing away from thick fire. We were left wondering and screaming because we had no idea if they made it to safety.

Yes, I know it was a fiction movie, but it was a really good fiction movie that ended in the worst way possible, without a clear concise conclusion. Don't you just hate that? I sure do, but let's get back to the good news.

It Gets Better

I'm not certain about a lot of things in my life, but I do have absolute certainty that regardless of how painful your experiences, it will get better. God will transform the bad memory into a new song—a song for good. He will give you beauty for your ashes, joy for your sadness, strength in your weakness, and hope when you feel helpless. You will not sing songs of despair your entire life, even if that seems like the song that has been on repeat for months or even years. You *will* sing songs of joy.

And while the memories are typically not wiped from our memories, they are no longer isolated events that exist. God will now be attached to those memories, though He was already attached, but we didn't quite know it. It's like basic math.

Event = Pain
Pain + God = A New Song

When you add God to the equation, there is a better outcome. There is a changed you as well as a better memory.

You will one day be brought to tears by how amazing God has been to you. You will one day be compelled to share with anyone willing to listen, just how God transformed your life and gave you a new song to sing. You will be brought to your knees by the memories of how God rescued you. Because how could you not jump for joy and sing about a God who relentlessly pursues you *and* saves you from the messiness of life?

Chapter 13

Rehearse & Repeat

Hi friends. Wow. We have reached the last chapter. I am surprised that we made it here. Not that I doubted God could do it, but through the writing of this entire book, I questioned why me. I questioned why God would use me and if I could even do this. The truth is I struggled through the entire process of writing this book. There were days when I wanted to give up and stop writing. There were days when I let satan have the upper hand and talk me away from moving forward. There were days that I let him speak louder than I let the voice of God speak. There were days when I cried because I felt incapable of completing such a task as writing a book about my life experiences and sharing it with the world.

It hasn't been easy, but I do pray that as you have read through the pages of this book you were able to resonate, laugh, cry, and smile a bit.

This chapter is completely on a whim, but it is so needed. It is a reminder and a token that I hope you take with you forever. *Rehearse and Repeat.*

We talked a little bit about rehearsing in the chapter titled "A Transformed Mind," but I have to address it again before we go. To rehearse something is to learn it, to commit it to memory, and to keep practicing it. When I was little, I played the piano and if I wasn't practicing during the week, my pieces were not all that great. I had to remember the notes, I had to remember the progression of chords, and I had to rehearse constantly so that the day of my recital I would be able to show off my hard work. It wasn't just an event for my immediate family. I was going to be playing in front of my entire church, so rehearsal was mandatory.

Rehearsal is going to be necessary in your life. I don't mean rehearsing sheet music for a piano recital, but I mean rehearsal of truth. Over and over and over again, you are going to have to rehearse and repeat the things that you've learned while reading. As I have said before, these chapters are in no particular order. They are no perfect solution to your pain and the despair you may be feeling, but they are nuggets that everyone can benefit from whether you are struggling in your darkest night or you are struggling with fear, anxiety, or grief. These are universal steps that can be used with whatever life circumstance you may encounter. And, friends, here is the truth.

You will have trials in this life according to John 16:33. You are not exempt from suffering. The scripture says trials, not *a* trial. Trials. That's plural.

So, yes, you may suffer again. You may get through one of the toughest times of your life and then months later go through something else. But once you go through it once, you know what to implore as you struggle again. And, no, not every thing that you go through in your life will look the same, but you can still fight the battle with the same tools that I've shared with you here: a transformed mind, community, the Word of God, and prayer.

I suffered tremendously as I wrote this book. I thought I had it bad in college, but another wave came when I graduated, and another and another and another. They don't stop, friends. The enemy does not and will not stop. If you have chosen to have a relationship with God, it is inevitable. Trials are going to happen because satan does not want you to succeed. He does not want believers to prosper because he didn't prosper. He was thrown from his heavenly home and now he wants everyone to suffer with him.

But even while all of this may be true, you have a friend, a fighter, a light in the darkness who cares for you. You have a friend who will never stop fighting for you and will never let you be shaken (Psalm 55:22 NIV). You have a friend who will never leave you nor forsake you (Deuteronomy 31:6 NIV). He is a friend at all times — a hiding place and a refuge.

There was a day where this truth was magnified in my life. I was laying on my bed staring at my ceiling and just thinking. I remember laying there and admiring the stillness and silence that I heard, and that is not normal where I live. I live in an apartment that is on the bottom floor, and if you look out the back window of my bedroom all you see is the woods. So, you can imagine that it gets noisy. Between the people upstairs who don't know how to walk without stomping, and the creatures I hear outside my window sometimes or the rustling of the trees and leaves, I don't revel in much silence. But this one morning I did. I heard not one peep. Not one rustling of leaves. Not one bird. Not one loud footstep.

I embraced it in that moment. I looked closer at my ceiling and I saw this black little dot. It wasn't above my head but a few feet away. I stood up and I saw a spider. I am not a fan of spiders at all, but this one I just looked at. I was curious, *where did you come from?* I imagine that he crawled in one of the tiny little cracks somewhere in my apartment because it had been raining the day before. But then God spoke to me through that little spider.

If you are willing to listen, God can speak to you through anything whether it's a pancake, oatmeal, a car, or a spider. What He told me was that in times of chaos and unideal situations, that spider came into a place where he was safe. Well the spider sort of assumed he would be safe. How did he know I wouldn't kill him? I do not like spiders at all, but I didn't kill this spider. God told me that the spider knew where to go when his or her life was in danger. But then he asked me do I know where to go? When things get crazy in my life and I feel like giving up and quitting, do I know where to go?

Well, now I do. I flee to God. I flee to my Father. And I'm not going to lie and act like I have it all together and do this perfectly after a couple trial runs. Sometimes I go to my freezer and grab an ice cream bar or some other food to stuff my face, *then* I run to God. But we have to rehearse and repeat this. Not the running to food first, but the running to God first in times of chaos and nonideal circumstances in our lives. He is the only answer. He always is and always should be. And He won't disappoint, friends.

And who knows, now that you know where to run, you might find yourself eventually asking for another trial because you realize just how great He is. I did...eventually.

Another Song

In 2019, a group called Maverick City Music released a song called "Refiner." Now I love Maverick City Music and all of the songs that they have released, but this one song, I couldn't listen to it. I couldn't sing it. It would pop up on my playlist and my mind said, *Nope, no thanks.* I wasn't having it. I would not allow myself to listen to it. If you have heard the song, you may understand my sentiment but if you have not, let me enlighten you. The lyrics to the pre-chorus and chorus talk about wanting to be refined, purified, and consumed by fire.

My immediate thought after hearing this song the first time was *what? Why would you say that? Why would anyone want that?* I couldn't hear those words. I didn't want to be purified or tried by fire. I wanted to live my life, serving God, free of pain, free of heartbreak, and free of trial. I was sick of the fires. I was sick of being refined. I just wanted a break from being a Christian so the trials could be on pause for a bit. I would've loved that. But that's not how a relationship with God works. Well, I could take a break but I would probably be worse off without Him.

For days I couldn't listen to the song. I just couldn't bring myself to let those words come out of my mouth because they weren't true. I would never say those things out of my mouth. Never say never, my friends.

I remember the day it happened. It's funny to me now that I think about it. The song popped up on my playlist and I started singing. Seconds later when I realized what I was singing I gasped and immediately grabbed my phone and again I said *No*. God was slick. He almost got me. He was so close. But days went on again. I listened to every song on the Maverick City Music volume 2 album, except "Refiner." But then God began to prune my heart. He began to reveal to me the closeness that I feel when I am with Him, and the closeness that I feel to Him when I am in a trial and walking through the fire, drowning in sadness, or stuck in the pit of despair. He began to show me and remind me how close I get to be to Him. And it's not to say that He is not close when we are not going through something because He is present there too. But oftentimes when we are in the thick of it and experiencing some pretty intense emotions, that's when we *can* feel Him the most.

So, friends, I sang that song. I sang that song with all my heart and asked God to refine me. I asked Him to walk me through the fire. I asked Him to come near. It wasn't easy, but I meant it with all my heart. And you may think I was overreacting, but words have so much power. The Bible says that life and death is in the power of the tongue (Proverbs 18:21, NKJV). What we say matters. So no, I didn't, and I couldn't sing the lyrics to that song at one point in my life. I couldn't say something that I really did not desire to happen.

And maybe you recognize a bit of fear or anxiety in your life regarding trials like I did. Maybe you walked out of the other side of your trial and you're bummed that it could happen again. Maybe you fear the next trial that is going to come. Maybe you are afraid of how strong or how long the next attack is going to be. Maybe you don't want the next trial to come.

I understand. I came from a place where I would fear that the shoe could drop at any moment. It's a place where I felt like certain things were "too good to be true," so I didn't fully allow myself to enjoy it. It's the place where I felt that at any moment my happiness and joy would be snatched from me. Oftentimes I still do have that belief. Oftentimes I still fear the moment that death and darkness will come knocking at my door again. I fear the next pit of despair.

However, what is the title of this chapter? I hope you didn't go back and look, but you remembered it. It is called "Rehearse and Repeat." Just as the trial and the violent winds may come back, we must go back to what we know. We must go back to the truth that we know to be true. We must go back to the truth that we have encountered and repeat the things that we have learned.

I wish I didn't have to tell you that trials will come back but they will, friends, and when it does you will be well equipped for it. You have every tool at your disposal that you need to fight the depression, the fear, the anxiety, or the anger. You just have to access it.

Before You Go

I'll end with this: yes, the storms will come, but so will the songs, and so will the dancing of joy in the rain, if that's your thing. I've always dreamed of dancing in the rain to Whitney Houston's "I Wanna Dance With Somebody," blasting from my car. It will happen one day. Maybe in my next book you'll hear all about it.

But the dancing, the laughing, and the remembering must also be rehearsed and repeated.

These trials aren't things we just get through. They are memories. Memories worth keeping and sharing and telling.

There are countless moments in the Bible that people practiced this. Though it may have looked different then, many people would make altars at specific places. They would dedicate a certain location to the Lord because of what He did at that place.

In Genesis 35:7 (NIV), Jacob built an altar and named it El Bethel, because it was there that God revealed Himself to him when he was fleeing from his brother. After Isaac was forced to leave his home in Genesis 16, the Lord appeared to Isaac and Isaac built an altar there. In Joshua 4, Joshua and the Israelites were instructed by the Lord to lay stones after they passed through the Jordan river on dry ground to serve as a memorial forever.

I'll forever remember the days sitting on my bathroom floor and the pain that I felt. I'll forever remember the days of crying my eyes out praying for a better day and the pain to go away. I will forever remember those days. But I will also always remember God's faithfulness to lift me in my despair. I will always remember the days of joy and gladness that followed. I will always remember crossing over to the other side of my pain, and that is worth rehearsing and repeating.

No, I don't have stones or anything to commemorate all of this, but I do have this book and journals commemorating every single mountain and valley that I have experienced. Well, maybe not all, but the majority of them.

I don't know how you like to keep track of your memories or if you write in a journal, but I do encourage you as the Lord did His people, to commemorate these moments. Commemorate your many victories so that you may never forget in your darkest night how God lifted you out of the mud and mire.

Acknowledgments

I never anticipated or imagined myself writing a book. I questioned God throughout this whole process wondering if He made a mistake or if He meant to choose me. I mean I'm sure there are a million other Brittany Roberts out there. But God makes no mistake, so here we are.

Obediently, I complete this last page before I hand over my story to be released to the world. However, I would be remiss to pass over all of those who have served as vessels to help me in this process.

To my family. Thank you for loving me unconditionally. Thank you for encouraging me and supporting me in ways that you may not even know. Thank you for never minimizing my pain and experiences but supporting me each step of the way. You all mean the world to me and I am so grateful for you! You have made me a better woman.

To my many sisters in Christ. Thank you for always speaking God's truth to me. Thank you for knocking some sense into me and keeping me accountable as I wrote. I am so grateful that God has surrounded me by women, by sisters like you, who genuinely care for me and always point me back to Jesus.

To my DUCC family. You all are amazing, and I am so grateful for you! From your initial pursuit of me as a college student, to your continuous pursuit and willingness to help me grow as a young woman, I truly would not be where I am today if it were not for you.

To God. Thank You. Thank You for seeing me as I am. Dirt and all but choosing to love me all the same. Thank You for this life that I am so unworthy of living. And thank You again for choosing me to share this message with your people.

www.ingramcontent.com/pod-product-compliance
Lightning Source LLC
Chambersburg PA
CBHW071437080526
44587CB00014B/1883